THE
JAM MAKER'S
GARDEN

GROW YOUR OWN SEASONAL PRESERVES

THE
JAM MAKER'S GARDEN

GROW YOUR OWN SEASONAL PRESERVES

HOLLY FARRELL

Photographs by **JASON INGRAM**

F FRANCES LINCOLN

Contents

From the fruit garden

From the veg garden

From the herb garden

Introduction

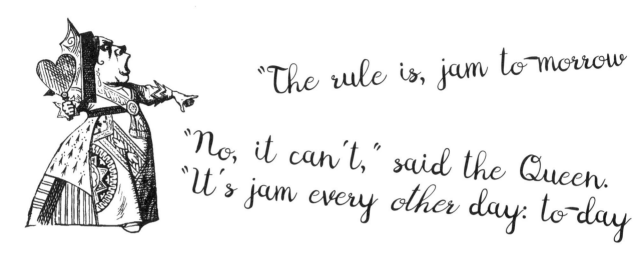

"The rule is, jam to-morrow

"No, it can't," said the Queen. "It's jam every other day: to-day

While this quote from Lewis Carroll's *Alice in Wonderland* always makes me smile, it also strikes fear into my heart. A world without jam is a terrible one. No jam for toast, cakes or scones? And, by extension, no chutney for a cheese sandwich or pickles for a burger? A sad world indeed.

Joking aside, a world without jam would be entirely different: the quest to preserve food is age old. In the past it was borne out of necessity, a means of furthering summer gluts through winter scarcity and bringing variety and nutrients to the winter diet, though the use of sugar also made it a luxury. As Michael Pollan writes in *Second Nature: A Gardener's Education*, 'Harvest's work is to hold off, at least temporarily, earth's corruptions, the spoilage of our spoils . . . Cooking, canning, freezing, acidifying . . . sugaring – the culture's time-tested prophylactics against nature's rot, ingenious tools of the "kitchen garden".'

These days we are lucky enough to be able to preserve because we want to rather than have to, yet jam making often gets a bad press. It is often used as shorthand for a small-town, small-world, small life, as if it is impossible to make jam and be engaged in international affairs at the same time. This book, in which I hope to inspire you to both garden and preserve, is hardly going to challenge jam making's image.

However, making jams and chutneys – and growing the fruit and vegetables to go in them – brings a connection with the seasons and nature that is not to be sniffed at. With the year-round availability of all manner of fruits and vegetables in a worldwide economy, the changing seasons are easily lost. That sweet, heady whiff of fruit on opening a jar of home-grown strawberry jam on a dull winter's day brings with it the promise of the summer and garden bounty to come. Even when fresh, an out-of-season strawberry just does not compare: there's a reason jam is known as bottled sunshine.

A home-made preserve has an inherent connection with people and place as well. Different seasons will produce variations in the crops – even from the same plant – depending on the sunshine, rainfall and all the other factors that go into creating the flavour of fruit and veg, and therefore the taste of the preserve. On opening a jar we can, like discussing vintages of fine wines, recall the superlative raspberry jam of '03, and hope for a similar result next year. A family member,

and jam yesterday but never jam to-day."

"It must come sometimes to 'jam to-day'," Alice objected.

isn't any other day, you know."

perhaps living on the other side of the world, can be instantly transported home by the taste of their favourite jelly received in the post. A jar given to a friend is a gift that is always welcome (perhaps where the fresh produce might not be!), for it is personal, not generic or made by machine.

When I started growing and preserving, I would gather any and all harvests possible from anywhere I could, partly out of a desire to avoid waste and partly out of the love of preserving. I ended up with a lot of jars of courgette chutney that I did not really like and now I am more selective. There is no point in growing a crop that you do not actually like to eat and, if you have, there is definitely no point in preserving it! Give it away and do not grow it again.

Growing and preserving should complement each other – two cycles perfectly in sync. That which we grow but cannot eat gets preserved to be eaten later when the plant is no longer cropping: we avoid waste and extend the harvest. By the time we have used up the preserve, the new season provides us with a fresh harvest again. When you preserve, there is no such thing as a glut.

Yet there is more to preserving than simply making something last longer. The fruit or vegetable – whatever it might be – is transformed in an alchemical process into a food that is more than the sum of its parts, and is a completely different entity from the original crop. It is possible to enhance the pure flavour or make it more complex. That said, in this book I have kept my focus firmly on my garden: using where possible fresh, home-grown ingredients such as herbs and flowers to add subtlety rather than exotic spices.

'The teeming autumn, big with rich increase . . .'
William Shakespeare (*Sonnet 97*)

Ultimately I make jam because I am greedy. It is not enough to savour the kitchen garden's harvests there and then; I have to have more to eat at a later date – and I always overestimate how much I will actually want through the year (though that does mean I always have plenty to give away). A line of gleaming jars on the kitchen shelf brings as much pleasure as a line of crops in the garden: there will be jam tomorrow *and* today.

BEFORE YOU START

I n the spirit of the harvest–preserve–harvest cycle (and because I think the fresh flavour of many jams and jellies deteriorates after a year or so), I have kept the quantities of each recipe in this book relatively low. I also think this better reflects the modern domestic fruit and vegetable garden, which favours variety over quantity.

My guiding principles in these recipes were that the garden produce had to shine, that the ingredients should be readily accessible and that they should taste amazing. The herbs, flowers and spices I have suggested as variations to some recipes are those that I think best enhance the flavour of the preserve and are most commonly available. However you should make the most of your plot. If you have a crop you think will work well, give it a go!

Likewise I have not included recipes for the more unusual (but increasingly obtainable) berries such as honeyberries, jostaberries, white strawberries, pineberries and fuchsia berries because I think these are more likely to be grown as curios and not in sufficient quantities for preserving. However if you do have a glut, find a recipe for the fruit that your plant most resembles and try substituting it in part or in whole.

I am not suggesting that you grow crops exclusively to preserve them. In fact I would be disappointed if you did, for you would be missing out on the pleasures of eating the fresh fruit or vegetables in season. I simply hope that both the Growing and Make pages in *The Jam Maker's Garden* inspire you with some different, and delicious, plants for your garden and their harvest. If you do not have enough of a crop to preserve in any year, seek out your local pick-your-own farm to bulk out your produce.

Throughout this book, measurements are given in metric and imperial – please use just one or the other, do not mix the two. Guidance on general techniques such as seed sowing and testing for a set is given in Garden notes (see page 10) and Kitchen notes (see page 24).

GARDEN NOTES

Preparation

All gardens begin with the soil. The more time you put into creating a lovely home for your plants before you put them in the soil, the more reward they will give you. Kitchen gardens for jam will have a natural inclination towards fruit bushes and trees, and with these long-term plantings you should get the soil right first time: it is better to put a 50p plant in a £5 hole than a £5 plant in a 50p hole.

THE SOIL

It is important to know what kind of soil you have, so do a quick test yourself or send a sample to the Royal Horticultural Society (see Further resources, page 171) for a full analysis. Clay soils will easily stick together and roll into a ball or even a sausage shape in your hand, while sandy soils feel gritty and do not stick together so well, if at all. Most soils fall somewhere in the middle of this spectrum, but all will be improved with an annual (or six-monthly) application of well-rotted organic matter.

COMPOST AND OTHER ORGANIC MATTER

Organic matter is any broken-down material that can be used as a soil improver or planting medium for pots. Compost (either home-made or bought) and well-rotted manure or mushroom compost are the most common forms. Note that 'organic matter' is not necessarily organic, that is, devoid of pesticides and other chemicals. Always buy the best-quality compost you can afford. For convenience, in this book all types of organic matter have been referred to as simply 'compost'.

For clay soils, organic matter will break up the soil to make it easier to work, and so that it does not bake

Add organic matter to the soil at least once every year: it will improve the health of the soil and therefore the health of your plants.

and crack into hard clumps in the heat. For sandy soils, the addition of organic matter will help the soil hold on to water and nutrients for longer. For all soils, it adds nutrition and soil flora and fauna – all vital for developing a healthy soil ecosystem in which your plants will thrive.

PREPARING SOIL FOR PLANTING

There are two schools of thought on soil preparation for kitchen gardens: the dig and no-dig camps. No-dig proponents (see the work of Charles Dowding) advise that, to preserve the delicate environment of the soil, it should be left well alone, and simply replenished with a layer of organic matter every year. Meanwhile the diggers turn over their whole plot every winter either by hand or with rotavators.

Many gardeners, myself included, steer a middle way, by leaving the soil as much as possible but digging when it needs some aeration. Certainly it is also worth digging over new areas, such as old lawn or a new allotment, to remove perennial weeds and relieve any compaction. Thereafter walk on the soil as little as possible and keep adding organic matter.

1. Clear the soil of any weeds, then spread a thick (around 10cm/4in) layer of organic matter over the whole plot.

2. Use a garden fork to incorporate the organic matter into the soil, digging it in as deep as the fork's tines. Remove the roots of any perennial weeds that were overlooked the first time.

3. Rake the soil surface roughly level. Then, with your feet together, shuffle over the whole plot. This consolidates (but does not compact) the soil and removes any large air pockets. If roots were to sit in large air pockets they would drown when the soil was wet or dry out in hot weather.

4. Rake again so the ground is level and has a fine tilth over the top. The children's author Julia Donaldson explains a good tilth perfectly in this rhyme, taken from *How Does Your Garden Grow*: 'Put down the spade. Pick up a rake. And rake it smooth as a crumbly cake.' You are now ready to sow or plant.

RAISED BEDS, POTS AND OTHER CONTAINERS

It is perfectly possible to grow a full range of fruit trees and bushes in raised beds and/or pots, providing they have a minimum depth of 45cm/18in. Fill raised beds with topsoil mixed with compost. If you use sterilized topsoil for the raised bed you will be thankful for the initial lack of weed seeds. Put multipurpose compost in pots and other containers, unless you are growing acid-lovers (see Growing blueberries, page 60). Growing plants in raised beds and pots suggests an intrinsic lack of space, so consider trained forms such as cordons, fans or espaliers, which leave more room for other plants and still give a good harvest.

Some tips on kitchen garden design

- Always try to keep your annual and perennial plants separate, to save disturbing the soil and roots of the perennial plants when planting and harvesting the annuals.
- Most fruit and vegetable crops prefer full sun, but there are still plenty of options for partial shade, such as currant bushes. If you have a few walls of different aspects on which you could train fruit trees/bushes, put the apples, pears, redcurrants or gooseberries on the north- and east-facing ones and the cherries and plums on the south- and west-facing walls.
- Utilize your space efficiently by adopting some of the principles of forest gardening (see Further resources, page 171): the top tier is your fruit trees, underneath those are the fruit bushes; and as ground cover plant herbs and flowers such as mint (*Mentha*), wild garlic (*Allium ursinum*) and sweet violets (*Viola odorata*).

Fruit trees

Buying a fruit tree is an investment, so it is good to get the right one! Choosing a variety is the fun part, but make sure you check that the rootstock and pollination groups fit the situation in which the tree is to grow before parting with your money.

Also consider whether you want to buy the tree bare rooted or potted. Potted trees are available year-round, but are more expensive. Bare-root ones are just that – they will have been planted in a box or bed of loose compost at the nursery and you lift it out and take it home with the roots covered by a bin bag (bare-root trees are also available online). They are available only when the trees are dormant in winter. It is sometimes possible to source a greater range of varieties as bare-root trees than potted ones.

ROOTSTOCKS

All fruit trees are supplied as grafted trees. That is, each one consists of two parts: a rootstock (root system) and a scion (the variety that has been grafted on to the rootstock). The properties of the rootstock (usually the tree's ultimate size, but the MM rootstocks also add disease resistance) are passed on to the scion variety. For example, an 'Egremont Russet' apple scion on an M25 rootstock could grow into a 6m/20ft tall tree, but on an M27 rootstock it could be trained into a 1m/3ft cordon. The more dwarfing the rootstock, the less vigorous and smaller the ultimate tree, so for a small cordon use M27 and for a larger one choose M9 or even M26.

POLLINATION GROUPS

Different fruit varieties flower at various times through the spring, and in order to get your tree's flowers pollinated (and therefore have fruit to harvest), it will need another tree nearby that is flowering at the same time. For each type of fruit – apples, pears, plums and cherries – there are a number of pollination groups, and you will require two varieties from the same or adjacent groups for good pollination.

However some fruits, and some varieties of fruits, are self-fertile, that is, they do not need another tree to be successfully pollinated (see the individual Growing pages).

There are also other ways to achieve pollination: a crab apple tree will act as a pollinator partner for all apple trees, and if your immediate neighbours have the same fruit trees as you these will also work.

THE MOST COMMON ROOTSTOCKS AND THEIR USES		
Apples	M27	Very dwarfing: small bush tree, cordon, stepover
Apples	M9	Dwarfing: small bush tree, cordon
Apples	M26	Semi-dwarfing: small bush tree, cordon
Apples	MM106	Semi-vigorous: small bush tree, espalier
Apples	MM111	Semi-vigorous: trees, bush tree, espalier, fan
Apples	M25	Vigorous: tree
Cherries	Gisela 5	Semi-dwarfing: small bush tree, fan
Cherries	Colt	Semi-vigorous: tree, bush tree, fan
Pears	Quince C	Semi-dwarfing: small bush tree, cordon, espalier, fan, stepover
Pears	Quince A	Semi-vigorous: tree, bush tree, cordon, espalier, fan
Plums	Pixy	Semi-dwarfing: small bush tree, cordon, fan
Plums	St Julien A	Semi-vigorous: tree, bush tree, fan

TRAINED FORMS

Training fruit trees is a great way to squeeze them into a small space and still get a decent harvest. All can be trained against a wall (good for providing a little extra warmth to the tree), a fence or as a free-standing screen. For training information see Pruning and training, page 17.

The simplest form of trained tree is a cordon – a single stem with very short fruiting lateral branches. A double cordon has two stems trained in a U-shape.

Stepovers are great for edging a plot and are either a cordon that is bent over in one direction, or a tree that has been allowed to form two branches that are bent over and trained in opposite directions.

An espalier has a central stem and horizontally trained lateral branches.

Fan-trained trees have no central stem but a number of branches trained diagonally off a short leg to form a fan shape.

Pruning and training

Each Growing page outlines the specific pruning requirements and potential training for that plant. Here are the general principles.

PRUNING BASICS

Pruning is carried out for a number of reasons: to restrict the size of a plant; to promote flowering and fruiting growth; and to create and maintain a good framework of healthy fruiting branches that allow light and air into the plant. Left to their own devices fruit trees and bushes will produce a harvest, but pruning maximizes it.

Of all garden tasks, pruning is easily the one that most gardeners are most afraid of. Fear not! It is really quite hard to kill a plant through bad pruning; the worst that could happen is that you do not get a crop that year, or it just looks as if the plant has had a bad haircut. And, just like bad haircuts, it will grow out eventually.

Whenever you are pruning, always cut or saw just above a bud, leaf or branching point. Even in winter buds are visible as raised bumps on a branch, stem or trunk. Cut as close as you can above the bud, without touching the bud itself. Straight cuts are fine when using secateurs. With a saw, leave a slight collar, that is, a tiny stump where the branch joins on to the larger branch or trunk. When removing large branches, make three cuts to avoid the branch tearing off. First make an incision underneath the branch, about 30cm/12in nearer the tip from where you want the final cut to be, sawing through half of the trunk. Then slightly above that cut, saw through from the top to remove most of the branch. Finally tidy up the stump to a neat collar.

THE 4DS

Before any other pruning, tackle the 4Ds: dead, dying, diseased and duplicate stems. Remove any dead, dying or diseased branches back to healthy wood, making sure that the cut is at least 10cm/4in into the healthy section. Duplicate branches – those that are crossing each other, rubbing together or growing the same way but one slightly higher than the other, should be pruned back to a suitable point.

Prune all branches just above a bud, to promote healthy, new growth and to avoid ugly, dead stubs.

SEASONAL PRUNING

Pruning in winter reduces the size of a plant and also promotes new growth to replace the old wood that has been removed. Additional summer pruning is done to restrict the growth of trained forms and to allow more light and air into the plant to aid ripening. Cherries and plums get their main pruning in summer to avoid spreading diseases, while most other fruit has at least winter pruning and sometimes winter and summer sessions (see the individual Growing pages).

FORMATIVE PRUNING

Young fruit trees do not need a lot of pruning in their first years, but a few strategic cuts now will create a good framework for the years to come. All plants have a chemical process known as apical dominance, which basically means the highest branch tip gets all the attention so it grows upwards to the sunshine as quickly as possible. By taking off this tip you can divert the process and promote branching and bushier growth, creating a better-shaped tree. All that is required is to shorten the trunk and any branches by about two-thirds of their total length after planting, and then by one-third in the following year. Thereafter prune as for a mature tree (see below).

TRAINING

To train a fruit tree into a particular shape – espalier, stepover, cordon or fan (see Trained forms, page 15) – always prepare your wires first, whether they be against a wall or between posts in the ground. Fix the wires using eyelet screws, and always make them as taut as possible. On the ground allow at least 75cm/30in between each cordon and single-stem stepover and at least a 3m/10ft spread between each fan or espalier. The branches of espaliers and fans should be 45cm/18in apart vertically. Always set the wires horizontally. When training branches diagonally (cordons at a 45 degree angle or in a fan shape), fix bamboo canes along the line you want the branch to follow to make tying in easier. Use a figure-of-eight tie with horticultural string, looping around the branch and then tying off the second loop against the wire.

Tie in the new growth in winter and summer, when pruning. At the same time, check all the previous year's ties, replacing and loosening as necessary. Be patient – trained forms take some time to get there, but it is worth getting it right. For example, you will be able to add another tier to an espalier only once a year. To speed things up, you could buy a tree on which the training has already been started, but if doing this always check it is subsequent years' growth (look for the pruning cuts) and not a single year's growth simply tied to a frame, which will ultimately not be as productive.

PRUNING A MATURE TREE

Having removed the 4Ds, any other pruning is to ensure that each free-standing tree has a good framework of branches. You are aiming to create a goblet shape: four or five larger branches around the edge, leaving an open area in the middle for good air circulation. Never remove more than one-quarter of the total growth at any one time.

Trained trees are pruned in summer, because this restricts growth more than cutting back in winter. Reduce each lateral coming off the main stem to three buds, and trim off the ends of branches that have reached the ends of their wires. It may also help to do a little winter pruning, just to thin out any large clusters of laterals.

Take out branches growing across the centre of the tree, to aid good air circulation.

Sowing and planting

BASIC PRINCIPLES

The size of each seed dictates how to sow it. In general, seeds should be covered with compost 2–3 times the depth of the seed itself. Small seeds therefore need only a light covering, and very fine ones are simply sprinkled on to the surface of the compost. Medium-sized and large seeds should be pushed deeper down into the soil.

For staggered harvests some crops can be sown in succession, but make sure you have enough for your preserves. Although it is often recommended to leave two weeks between sowings, it is much better to let the seeds themselves be your guide. Once the first/previous batch of seeds have germinated and put on their first true leaves (that is, the second pair of leaves; the first pair to appear after germination are the seed leaves and do not look like the leaves on the mature plant), it is time to sow the next batch. This method takes the vagaries of the weather into account and encourages a more even harvest over a long period.

Always check each seed packet for any sowing instructions specific to that plant, such as soaking the seed prior to sowing. Also always water the soil or compost thoroughly before sowing rather than after, to avoid washing the seeds out of place.

SOWING DIRECT INTO THE SOIL

By far the easiest method is to sow the seeds directly where you want them to grow. This is also the best option for root crops and other plants that dislike their roots being disturbed, such as carrots and sweetcorn.

There are two ways of sowing direct: in drills and in stations. Drills are long lines scraped out of the soil (to the correct depth, see Basic principles, above) into which the seeds are sprinkled finely ('thinly') and covered over. This method is best for crops that can be thinned as they develop, and the thinnings used in the kitchen, such as carrots and beetroot.

Sowing in stations is better for plants that need more space between them, such as sweetcorn, pumpkins and cauliflowers. Use a dibber (a pencil works fine) to make a hole in the soil to the correct depth, drop in a couple of seeds and cover over with more soil. Keep the soil moist until the seeds have germinated, then thin to the strongest seedling.

Drill sowing

Station sowing

SOWING UNDER COVER

For crops that need to be started early and cannot be planted out until after the last frosts, such as tomatoes and cucumbers, you need to sow the seeds and grow them on under cover, in a greenhouse or on a sunny windowsill. It is best to sow such seeds in the individual cells of a modular seed tray so each one develops a small clump of soil around its roots. Then, when you come to pot it on or plant it out, its young roots will be protected by the soil 'plug' and so will not be disturbed too much. Either buy plastic modular seed trays to fill with compost or make your own mini-pots using a paper potter (see box, page 20). Use a proprietary seed compost or a sieved multipurpose one, because young seedlings grow better in a lump-free potting medium.

Cover the seed trays/pots with clear plastic to help retain the heat and speed up germination. Remove the cover once the seedlings start to appear, to avoid excess humidity and thereby rot.

THINNING AND POTTING ON

Galling as it can be to remove potential plants, thinning is necessary to ensure healthy and strong growth so that the plants provide a decent harvest. Thin each cell, pot or station to the strongest-looking seedling, remembering that a short, stocky plant is better than a tall, leggy one. Gradually remove drill-sown seedlings until they are at their final specified spacing.

Seedlings raised under cover will probably outgrow their cells or pots before it is time to plant them out. They therefore should be potted on, into individual small pots (a 9cm/3½in diameter pot is fine). Multipurpose compost is fine for this stage. When potting on be careful to hold only the root ball and the leaves, never the delicate stem of the seedling. Paper pots can be planted pot and all in the larger container, but make sure no paper is visible above the soil surface (tear off a bit if necessary) because this can act as a wick and draw moisture away from the roots. Water the plants well after potting on.

Pot on seedlings to give them more room to grow before they are ready to plant out.

MAKING PAPER POTS

1. Roll long strips of newspaper around the pot-maker, to form the sides of the pot. There is no need to stick down the end.

2. Fold over the paper ends so the pot-maker base is covered, then grind them on to the base, to secure. Pull the pot off the maker.

3. Fill each pot with compost and water, then sow your seeds. When ready they can be potted on or planted, newspaper and all.

HARDENING OFF

Whether home-grown or bought, tender young plants can be put outside into the soil or a larger pot once all risk of frost has passed. This is usually in late spring or early summer. Before doing this, however, it is essential to harden off your plants by putting them outside in their pots just for the daytime for about a week, then during the nights as well for a few days before planting them permanently outside. This allows each plant to acclimatize to the cooler temperatures and avoids any shock to its system that might check its growth for a while.

PLANTING POTTED PLANTS

For young vegetable plants, dig holes at the spacings specified in the Growing pages, then put one plant in each and refill the hole around the root ball. Ensure each root ball is properly firmed into the soil/compost, but do not press down around the base of the stem, because this can break off the delicate roots. Water in well and continue to water for a week or so, until the plants have had a chance to establish properly in their new position.

For more mature plants such as potted herbs, dig a hole about one and a half times the size of the current pot, before planting as above.

PLANTING BUSHES AND TREES

Soak bare-root plants in a bucket of water for twelve or so hours before planting. Water container-grown plants well. Dig a hole twice the size of the pot or root-width (for bare-root plants), but not much deeper. If the ground seems compacted at the base of the hole, loosen it slightly with a garden fork. If a potted plant is badly root-bound, tease out a few of the roots where possible to help it establish. Some nurseries recommend using mycorrhizal fungi; this is a powder that purportedly helps roots to establish faster in the soil. If your soil is healthy anyway, it is probably not needed, but, if you are using it, it must be rubbed directly on to the roots or it will not work.

Young fruit trees can benefit from staking for at least a year – especially in exposed conditions – to prevent the stems breaking. Therefore drive a strong post into the planting hole and put the tree as close as you can to the stake. Keep the stake downwind of the tree (for

Bare-root plants can dry out in transit, so soak them in a bucket of water before planting.

Pests, diseases and other problems

The majority of potential infestations and infections can be avoided by cultivating a healthy plot. A soil ecosystem that works well will help to keep the plants healthy from beneath, and do its own battle against any soil-borne diseases or pests. Adopt a minimum-dig approach (see Preparing soil for planting, page 12), and apply good-quality compost at least once a year. Above ground, clear away old crops and keep weeds down to allow plenty of light and good air circulation around plants. Ensure pots and tools are clean too.

Proper watering and feeding prevent plants from becoming stressed, and a weaker plant is more likely to succumb to pests and diseases. If you are buying plants, check them over thoroughly before purchase (including turning them out of the pot to examine the roots), and do not buy anything that looks suspect. If you are purchasing online, make sure the retailer has a no-quibbles return policy so that you can send back sub-standard plants.

Get nature on your side too. Every garden has some pests, so the trick is to harbour their predators and tolerate a little damage in order to maintain enough of a population of the pests to keep the predators in residence. Birds, bugs (such as ladybirds and hoverflies) and amphibians (frogs, toads and newts) are all allies in the war against aphids, slugs and snails, so create a diverse environment with plenty of flowers, hiding places and even a small pond to keep them happy.

If you are using any sprays, always check the waiting time between application and harvest, and do not apply to flowers that you will be gathering, such as roses.

Finally there is no substitute for constant vigilance and fast action. As soon as you notice a problem, deal with it. Prompt removal of infected branches, or even a single leaf, can stop an infection or infestation in its tracks. For details on where to find guidance about pests and diseases specific to individual crops, and how to deal with them, see Further resources (page 170).

the prevailing wind) where possible, but if aesthetics dictate otherwise that is fine. Fasten the tree to the stake securely with a cushioned tie, and check the tie regularly to see if it needs loosening as the tree grows.

Put the plant in the hole so that its crown is at soil level. Then backfill around the roots/root ball, using your heel to firm it in properly. Rake once you have finished to neaten it up. Water the area really thoroughly, and continue watering well (as required – always check the soil) for a few weeks until the plant gets a chance to establish. A mulch of compost will help to keep the moisture in the soil.

Make the hole for each potted plant roughly twice as wide as its root ball.

Other garden tasks

WATERING

Getting watering right comes down to one simple rule: always check the soil first. Only by doing this can you know how much water the plant needs. Just judging by eye can be deceiving – a dry crust on top of the soil may conceal plenty of moisture below, or a short spell of rain might have wetted the surface but not any deeper. The same applies to pots. Generally you should aim for moist but not wet soil (though of course immediately after watering the soil/compost will be wet). It is particularly important not to let soil dry out while the plant is flowering and producing fruit, because this can cause flowers to drop prematurely, and fruit to swell irregularly.

Stick your finger into the soil or compost to check whether it needs watering. Then, if water is required, always soak the soil thoroughly, because this reduces the number of times you have to water. A little splash will not only be used up or evaporate quickly but also encourage the roots to grow to the surface, where they will only dry out faster. Water the soil surface rather than the plant; it is the roots not the leaves that need the water, and too much moisture on the foliage can create humidity that will foster disease.

FEEDING

Most plants benefit from the application of extra nutrients, whether it is just an annual mulch of compost, or a liquid fertilizer boost every two weeks. Fruit trees and bushes fall into the former camp, while annual vegetables are in the latter, but check the individual Growing pages for more details. Plants grown in pots need more fertilizer than those in the soil, but only from spring to late summer. Make sure at least one watering in four is pure water to avoid a build-up of salts in the compost.

Controlled-release (also known as slow-release) fertilizers tend to be granular. Rake these into the soil surface or mix with the backfill when planting. Avoid fertilizer plugs, which are pushed into the soil, because they do not break down as they are supposed to. For a more instantaneous boost use liquid fertilizers, which should be applied regularly over the growing season. Follow the instructions on the packet or bottle and do not be tempted to exceed them or you may poison the plants with an overdose. Organic options are available for both granular and liquid fertilizers.

WEEDING

Weeds are either annual plants, which germinate, flower, set seed and die within a year, or perennials, which come back year on year. Some blighters are even ephemeral, meaning they can have several generations of plants flowering within a growing season. Knowing which is which helps to deal with them; for some of the most common weeds and their growth habits, see the box opposite.

With annuals, preventing flowering is the main task when weeding. They can be hoed off, the younger the better, or hand weeded; and once removed you do not have to worry about them any more. Perennial weeds on the other hand develop extensive root systems, which means that simply pulling the top off will not kill the whole plant, and it will keep coming back until you remove the whole root. This can involve digging very deep (if you do not want to resort to weedkillers), unless you get them out as soon as possible when they first appear.

Keep on top of this crucial task by doing five minutes here and five minutes there, so it is not onerous. By viewing weeding as an opportunity to give your plants a health check at the same time, you are more likely to catch pests and diseases early (see Pests, disease and other problems, page 21). Always remove all weeds before they flower and set seed – and then spread around the garden creating more weeds. If you are short of time, just snap off the flower and come back for the rest later. Using ground-cover plants over bare soil will also help to suppress weeds in the first place (see Some tips on kitchen garden design, page 13).

COMMON WEEDS

Dandelion (*Taraxacum officinale*): perennial

Dock (*Rumex obtusifolius*): perennial

Creeping buttercup (*Ranunculus repens*): perennial

Annual meadow grass (*Poa annua*): annual or ephemeral

Hairy bittercress (*Cardamine hirsuta*): annual or ephemeral

Groundsel (*Senecio vulgaris*): annual

Stinging nettle (*Urtica dioica*): perennial

Fat hen (*Chenopodium album*): annual

Field horsetail (*Equisetum arvense*): perennial

KITCHEN NOTES

- *Conserve* Made with the whole fruit, as for a jam, but the fruit is steeped in sugar before cooking, only briefly, so the final set is softer with more intact fruit.

Definitions

To paraphrase Shakespeare: what's in a name? A jam by any other name would taste as sweet. All preserves are variations on a theme of cooked fruit/vegetables and sugar or vinegar, but in order to avoid any confusion here are my definitions of the various preserves in this book.

- *Compote* A compote has the lowest sugar level of any sweet preserve, and therefore must be kept in the refrigerator and eaten within a few days of making. Essentially it is stewed fruit.

- *Jam* This, the simplest of the preserves, is fruit and sugar boiled together until set into a soft consistency. The fruit is usually cooked alone first, then the sugar added for a final boil.

- *Jelly* Has a similar final consistency to jam, but is made with only the juice of the fruit, resulting in a clear, smooth product. Not to be confused with the US application of the word jelly, meaning a jam preserve.

- *Curd* A cooked, thick-set fruit custard most commonly made with citrus fruits, which will last for a month or so in the refrigerator.

- *Ketchup* Traditionally a sauce made with a single vegetable or fruit cooked with vinegar and sieved to a smooth consistency. Modern ketchups sometimes combine more than one vegetable/fruit.

- *Marmalade* A jam that generally includes citrus fruits and sometimes their peel, which is softened by lenghty cooking. Good marmalades have a bitter edge to their sweetness.

- *Pickle* Fruits or vegetables preserved in a salted or sugared vinegar. Generally the prettiest of the savoury preserves.

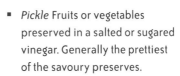

- *Relish* Although a relish may have virtually the same ingredients as a chutney, these are cooked only briefly so the vegetables or fruit retain more bite. They do not keep as long as a chutney.

- *Cheese* A strained jam that is boiled and dried to the extent that it can be set in a mould and sliced.

- *Syrup* The simplest syrup is a sugar solution in which herbs or flowers are steeped to release their flavour. Syrups can also be made with fruit juices, typically of berry fruits.

- *Chutney* The longest-cooked of the savoury preserves, chutneys have a sweet/sour taste and a sticky consistency. They need to mature before they can be eaten. I favour distinct chunks of fruit and veg (rather than an amorphous mass) and a 'single origin' approach (rather than throwing in the whole garden).

Ingredients: Your harvest

PREPARING YOUR HARVEST

The sooner you can preserve your fruit and vegetables after harvest, the better. All the recipes assume each piece of fruit or vegetable has been washed, dried and picked over (removing leaves, stalks and any wildlife). Most weights accommodate any subsequent peeling, coring, topping and tailing or pitting that might be necessary, but a few use the prepared weight.

Do not worry unduly about getting the weights absolutely accurate for the fruit and vegetable element. I tend to add a few grams to allow for discarding any bad bits that I might discover when chopping, but if I do not find any I eat a bit instead!

FREEZING FRUIT

Some fruits freeze well, and this is a good way to preserve them temporarily until you have time to

This crab apple is *Malus × moerlandsii* 'Profusion'.

make them into jam or decide what to do with them. When cooking with such frozen food, the weight of frozen fruit should be equal to that of the fresh fruit quantity specified. You can successfully freeze all berries (except strawberries) – and currants and chillies too. Lay the washed and dried fruit on a baking sheet, not touching, and put in the freezer for twenty-four hours before scraping them off the tray and into a freezer bag or airtight box for longer-term storage. When cooking jams and jellies, the fruit can be used straight from the freezer (just remember it will take a little longer to cook than from fresh). If you defrost it first (the better option for preserves like curds), use all the juices as well as the fruit itself.

PECTIN LEVELS

Perhaps the most off-putting part of jam making is its chemistry. To set and keep well, jam or jelly needs to have the fruit, sugar, acid and pectin levels at the right ratios. Pectin is a natural substance found in the fruit itself, particularly in the cores as well as stones and pips. When pectin is combined with acid – such as in fruit juice – and sugar, it will set jam. Low-pectin fruits such as strawberries often have acidic lemon juice added, to help them set. It is also possible to buy powdered and liquid pectin, and 'jam sugar' – sugar with added pectin – to help the set. The recipes in this book have been formulated to avoid these where possible.

ZESTING

That lovely aroma when you zest citrus fruit is from the essential oils in the skin being released. Aim to get as much of that oil into whatever it is you are making – either by zesting with a hand-held grater and holding it directly over (in, even) the pan, or by using a box grater out of which the condensed oil can be scraped. Always finely grate the rind, unless otherwise stated. The peel, when needed, is best pared from the fruit using a small, sharp knife. If you are buying citrus fruit, make sure that it is labelled as unwaxed.

OPPOSITE Most tree fruits, including crab apples, are ready for picking when the stalk breaks easily from the branch.

Caster sugar

Light muscovado sugar

Granulated sugar

Dark muscovado sugar

Golden granulated sugar

Demerara sugar

Ingredients: The rest

SUGAR

Pouring an entire bag of sugar into a jam pan is almost guaranteed to prompt vague thoughts of eating more healthily in future or else worries about that next trip to the dentist. Yes, preserving does involve a lot of sugar: but without it you would not be able to make preserves last so long, or taste so good! Do not be tempted to reduce the quantities specified; it will result in unsatisfactory setting and keeping. Jam is a luxury and should be treated as such – a little goes a long way. Refrigerator jams are the exception, but their lower sugar content means they rely on the cold temperatures to help preserve them, and they do not last as long.

There are different types of sugar, from dark, brown muscovado to pure white caster. Generally the darker the sugar, the less refined it is and the more treacly or caramel-like the flavour. Sometimes this complements a preserve, while at other times it overwhelms it, so again please use the sugar specified for the best results. (See also Pectin levels, page 26, on jam sugar).

Fresh herbs and flowers can be used to flavour sugar. I have only suggested such scented sugars in the recipes, rather than specifying them, because they take a while to mature and I wanted you to be able to preserve a harvest straightaway, without any forethought. I've suggested where they might be used in some recipes, but experiment with your own flavour combinations too.

VINEGARS AND SPICES

When buying vinegar and spices, always choose the best quality you can afford, and always use the correct vinegar as specified in the recipe because the acid content – and flavour – varies hugely between the different types. Cider vinegar, white and red wine vinegars and balsamic vinegar are the only ones included in this book, and all are widely available.

Spices are used either whole or ground, depending on the cooking time and whether the final product needs a clarity that ground spices would ruin. Ideally make your own ground spices from the whole ingredient (in a pestle and mortar, or an electric spice grinder). However the quality of bought ground spices is pretty good these days provided that they have not been at the back of the cupboard for years! Mixed spice, not to be confused with allspice, is a blend of various spices including cinnamon, coriander and usually nutmeg and/or cloves: source your preferred brand/blend.

MAKING SCENTED SUGARS

Scented sugars are a great thing to have in the cupboard, and a lovely gift in their own right.

To make a scented sugar, take a clean, dry jar and put a layer of caster or granulated sugar in the base. Add a layer of leaves or flowers (see below), and cover with more sugar. Repeat until you reach the top of the jar, finishing with a layer of sugar. Seal and store in a cool, dry place for at least a month before using, to allow the flavours to infuse the sugar.

Suitable garden candidates for making scented sugars include rosemary (*Rosmarinus*), thyme (*Thymus*) (try lemon thyme/ *T. citriodorus*), lavender (*Lavandula*) flowers, rose petals, scented pelargonium leaves and lemon verbena (*Aloysia citrodora*).

Equipment and sterilizing

WHAT YOU WILL NEED

I would like to debunk the theory that jam making requires a lot of specialized equipment (and therefore space in the cupboard). It does not. You do not even need a special pan, if you have already got a large saucepan. Of course there are a couple of things that would make life easier, but it would be fine to put them on your Christmas list and get preserving in the meantime. After all, humans were preserving food long before digital thermometers and suchlike were invented.

For most of the preserves in this book, you will probably already have most of the equipment you need in your kitchen. Your pan should be able to hold at least 5 litres/8¾ pints; while the initial ingredients might not come far up the sides, a jam can increase to several times its original volume when boiling. Jam, or maslin, pans are designed not only with this large volume in mind, but also with a heavy base and generally in stainless steel to conduct the heat evenly without the jam burning on to the base of the pan. Wooden spoons are better than metal, which can affect the flavour (especially of curds), although they will stain; alternatively use silicone spoons/spatulas. I keep separate spoons for sweet and savoury preserves to avoid flavour contamination.

Straining fruit and vegetables is often done through a sieve (note: always wash up the sieve or at least put it into soak as soon as possible after using, or it can be a nightmare to clean). For jelly making, the fruit pulp is left to drip through a fine mesh. This can be a specialist jelly bag, of which the cheaper nylon ones do the job absolutely perfectly, or else a large piece of muslin cloth tied up at the corners. (When we were doing the images for this book the photographer, Jason, asked if I would be suspending the bags over upturned chairs. As much as this would make a good picture, I had to disappoint him. I simply tie up the bags to a cupboard handle and leave them to drip into a bowl on the work surface. You can get a butcher's hook to make this easier, or tie the bag on to the jam-pan handle if it has notches so that the handle can be stood vertically and the bag sits well clear of the base.)

You will need measuring equipment too: scales – electronic scales are the most accurate, especially for small quantities; measuring jugs, preferably a big one and a little one for smaller quantities; and a sugar thermometer is a good investment. The last item is not necessary (see Testing for a set, page 32), but it does make life easier, as does a potting funnel. Thereafter how much you succumb to the kitchenalia shops and catalogues is up to you.

STERILIZING JARS AND BOTTLES

Incorrect washing and sterilizing can result in mould forming in stored preserves, so it is worth spending a few minutes making sure that your jars are scrupulously clean and properly sterilized.

The jars and bottles you use, especially if you are giving preserves as gifts, can affect the look of the jam enormously. A huge variety of shapes and sizes are available, and for that reason the recipes in this book give the final quantity of jam as a simple measurement, so you can work out which of your jars would add up to that total the best.

It is obviously worthwhile recycling jars where you can, but I would avoid using jars that previously had particularly pungent bought sauces in them as these inevitably transfer lingering flavours into the new contents. Similarly, when reusing your own jars it is best to avoid a jar for jam that previously had a chutney or pickle in it, and vice versa.

Wash jars really thoroughly in hot, soapy water, even though they were clean when you put them away, then rinse very thoroughly as well. Sterilizing is as simple as putting the jars in the oven at 110°C/225°F/gas mark ½ when you start prepping your ingredients. Turn the oven off after fifteen minutes but leave the jars in so they will be warm when you come to pot up your preserves (but not hot – if they are hotter than the preserve it will continue cooking). Alternatively put the jars in the dishwasher on its hottest cycle, and take them hot (but dry) out of the dishwasher straight to potting. None of the recipes requires sterilizing the filled jars/bottles. This is just too much of a faff to warrant being able to store something for an extra couple of months.

Testing, potting and storage

TESTING FOR A SET

Setting point is defined as the temperature at which, once cooled, a jam or jelly will solidify into a spreadable consistency. There are three ways to check this: temperature; the flake test; and the wrinkle test. Whichever method you use is up to you, but the more experienced you get at making jams, the more often you will know simply from the look and feel of the liquid that it is ready. Personally I rely on this gut instinct, backed up by a sugar thermometer and the wrinkle test (I am a belt-and-braces kind of girl).

Temperature

Setting point as indicated by a sugar thermometer is 105°C/221°F. Many thermometers handily have 'JAM' written on them at this point. Put the thermometer in the pan as soon as you start boiling and keep it there. Beware though that higher-pectin jams will set at a few degrees below this and that, when making small quantities, thermometers are not always accurate (that is, the jam may be at setting point even though the thermometer is reading well under 105°C/221°F). Digital thermometers can also be used, providing they are waterproof.

Flake test

Essentially this is a wrinkle test on a spoon, and it is a good initial indicator of setting point if you do not have a thermometer. Take the pan off the heat, to avoid overboiling, while you test the jam or jelly by coating a wooden spoon in the liquid and lifting it out of the pan; then spin the spoon around a few times to cool down the jam or jelly before letting it drop off the spoon (back into the pan – do not waste it). A jam at setting point will collect together and fall off as flakes, rather than run off in a continuous stream.

Wrinkle test

Put a saucer in the freezer as soon as you start making the jam or jelly. Once you think it is approaching setting point (as indicated by either or both of the above), take the pan off the heat and drop a small spoonful of jam or jelly on to the cold saucer and leave it for a minute or two. Once it has cooled a little, push the edge of the blob with your finger. If the surface wrinkles up it is ready for potting.

To do the wrinkle test, drop a spoonful of jam on to a cold plate and push the edge of the jam with your finger. If the surface wrinkles then it is at setting point.

SCUM

Not the nicest of words to associate with food, scum forming on the top of preserves as they boil is simply the impurities in the sugar and fruit cooking out. It is perfectly edible, but makes the jam look cloudy and unattractive if it is left in. Once setting point has been reached, scoop out the scum with a large spoon. A slotted spoon is usually specified, but I find these ineffective. A solid spoon means you sacrifice a little good jam, but it is worth it for a clean and quick scoop.

POTTING

Fill your warm, sterilized jars to 1cm/½in below the rim. For pickles and other preserves that will have vinegar poured over them once in the jar you should allow for a clear 1cm/½in vinegar plus another 1cm/½in of space below the rim – likewise for pesto, leave space for a layer of oil on top.

If you are using a jar with a screw-top or clip-top with a rubber seal, there is no need to add a wax disc, which personally I find fiddly and annoying. However,

Fill your warm, sterilized jars to 1cm/½in below the rim.

if you are only tying a piece of tautened cellophane over the top of the jar, the wax disc should be laid on the surface of the jam or jelly to seal it from the air (that is, the bacteria in the air) more effectively.

STORING PRESERVES

Store your preserves, unless otherwise stated, in a cool, dry, dark place because excess heat or light can cause discoloration and other problems. Once opened, some preserves must be kept in the refrigerator. Most jams and jellies however will not go mouldy very quickly and if you eat them fast enough you can avoid the refrigerator, which can dull their flavour (continue keeping them in the cool, dark place though). Mould forming on the top of unopened preserves is a result of unwanted bacteria in the jar: make sure the jars are properly washed, sterilized and warmed next time.

Try to eat your preserves within a year – not only will you have fresh ingredients for a new batch next year, but I find they taste best within this time frame.

SETTING PROBLEMS

- *Jam not set* Probably because the setting point was not reached. Pour it back in the pan and start cooking again.
- *Jam too stiff* This could be due to too much pectin in the mix, but more likely it is down to overcooking. Always use ripe fruit to counteract the former problem; for the latter mark it down to experience.
- *Crystallization* (solid lumps of sugar in the cooled jam, pictured above). This can be caused by overcooking, but also by not allowing the sugar to dissolve fully before starting to boil the combined mixture.
- *Shreds, fruit or pips all at the top* An uneven distribution in the cooled jam/marmalade is down to not letting it stand and not re-stirring before potting.
- *Chutney has a pool of liquid at the top* Insufficient cooking. Tip it out and cook for a bit longer.
- *Chutney is too dry* Overcooking. Try taking out as much as you want to use, and stirring in a little water before eating.

FROM

THE FRUIT
❯❯ GARDEN ❮❮

SPRING AND SUMMER

Growing strawberries

Almost any home-grown strawberry tastes better than shop-bought, if only because it has ripened fully on the plant. Picking in season and in the sunshine helps – get the fruit to the kitchen (if you can resist eating them) as quickly as possible to preserve as much of that warm summer's day aroma as possible.

BEST VARIETIES

Strawberry varieties are split into groups according to their harvest time: early, mid- and late season, with a fourth group (perpetual, or everbearing) that produces fruit all summer, although fewer at any one time. For preserving, it is best to have several plants producing at once, so choose appropriately depending on how much space you have. For early season berries try 'Honeoye'; for mid-season 'Cambridge Favourite' or 'Marshmello'; and then the late 'Malwina'. 'Mara des Bois' is the best perpetual.

PLANTING

The cheapest way to purchase plants is as cold-stored runners, usually available online or from nurseries in inexpensive bundles of ten or so. Otherwise buy module- or pot-grown plants. They grow in most soils or containers in a sunny position, but avoid the specific terracotta 'strawberry pots' with the openings down the side because these are a nightmare to water. Plant in autumn or early spring, ensuring the crown of the plant (where the roots meet the shoots) is exactly at soil level. It is possible to plant through plastic sheeting, which warms the soil and suppresses weeds, but it is very difficult to keep the plants well-watered (and the sheeting looks hideous to boot).

MAINTENANCE

Mulch and feed in spring. Water to keep the soil moist, especially during flowering and fruiting, but take care to direct the water on to the soil not the plant. This is to help prevent a fungal disease called *Botrytis* (grey mould) taking hold. Removing any rotting fruit or dead foliage promptly and cutting back all growth to the ground after fruiting will also help. Protect the ripening berries from birds – or in my case the dog – with netting. A mulch of straw as the fruit begins to ripen will keep the berries off the soil, but can harbour slugs and snails – make your choice.

After fruiting the plants will produce runners (long stems with little plantlets spaced along them), which grow out in search of new soil into which to root. Peg the first plantlet on each stem down into the soil and cut off the rest of the runner. Do this for 2–3 runners per plant and, once they have rooted, sever the stems from the main plant. You can then dig them up and move them in spring. Strawberry plants are best replaced every 3–5 years, so keep a good stock rotation by retaining some of these free plants each year.

HARVEST

When the berries are red and juicy, pick in the heat of the sun to ensure the flavours are at their maximum concentration.

Use in:

- Strawberry jam (page 38)
- Berry refrigerator jam (page 71) • Berry cordials and syrups (page 64)

Strawberry jam

The only jam to eat with scones and clotted cream – no store cupboard is complete without it. I prefer the odd whole strawberry to persist in the final jam, but if you want a smoother texture simply mash all the fruit. Strawberries are low in pectin, and produce a looser jam than other fruits, though it is still perfectly spreadable. For a firmer set, simply substitute jam sugar for granulated.

MAKES ABOUT 1.1KG/2LB 6OZ

INGREDIENTS
- 1kg/2lb 3oz hulled strawberries
- 850g/1lb 14oz granulated sugar
- 1½ lemons, juiced

METHOD
- Halve or quarter any larger strawberries. Then put all the fruit in a large ceramic or glass bowl and stir in the sugar. Cover and leave at room temperature for at least 8 hours, or overnight.
- Put the fruit and sugar into a large pan and mash roughly – leaving some or no berries whole as preferred – then stir in the lemon juice.
- Bring to a gentle simmer over a low–medium heat, stirring to dissolve the sugar, then simmer for 5–10 minutes until the fruit is soft.
- Turn up the heat and boil rapidly until the setting point is reached (see Testing for a set, page 32).
- Scoop out any scum, then leave to stand for 15 minutes. This prevents any large pieces of fruit floating to the top of the jar.
- Stir, then pot into warm, sterilized jars.

Grow
- Strawberries (page 36)
- Citrus: lemons (page 101)
- Thyme (page 157)

Store in a cool, dry, dark place
Keeps for a year or more

Something a little different

THYME
Thyme (*Thymus*) gives a lovely floral edge to strawberries.
- Stir through 1 tbsp fresh thyme leaves when adding the lemon juice.

BALSAMIC VINEGAR
One of my favourite ways to eat fresh strawberries is with a drizzle of balsamic reduction, so it made sense to add the flavour to the jam as well.
- Add 1 tbsp balsamic vinegar (or more to taste) when stirring in the lemon juice. The extra acidity makes for a slightly firmer set.

Growing gooseberries

According to the Royal Horticultural Society (RHS), there have been more than 3,000 gooseberry cultivars since the 1700s and around 150 cultivars are still grown, yet as fruit gooseberries are hardly ever seen in the shops. Help to keep these old varieties alive by planting a bush or two. As with all soft fruit, they take very little input for a large harvest every year and provide plenty for preserving and eating fresh.

BEST VARIETIES

Gooseberry varieties are generally split into dessert and culinary groups, with the former the only ones you would want to eat fresh off the plant. However by adopting a two-stage harvest system (see right), you can have plenty to preserve as well as to eat fresh from a single plant.

'Greenfinch' and 'Invicta' are both reliable culinary varieties and have some resistance to powdery mildew. Dessert gooseberry 'Leveller' develops a great flavour, while 'Whinham's Industry' bears red (rather than the usual acid green) berries.

PLANTING

Gooseberries tolerate most soils except poorly drained ones, and also crop well in partial shade, though they prefer full sun. They flower early, so avoid planting in frost pockets or you will lose your potential crop to the cold. When grown as standard bushes, gooseberries require an area of 1.5sq m/16sq ft for each plant (or a large pot), but they can also be trained as cordons or fans (see Trained forms, page 15).

MAINTENANCE

Water well in dry periods and as the plant is establishing, especially during flowering and as the fruits begin to swell. A well-watered plant is also less susceptible to powdery mildew. An annual mulch with compost in spring and an application of controlled-release fertilizer will also keep the plant healthy. If caterpillars appear, pick them off: the gooseberry sawfly will make short shrift of the plant's leaves, and weaken it for the following year.

Prune gooseberry bushes in early spring before the leaves appear to create an open goblet framework of around ten branches. Cut back last year's new shoots to two buds from the main stem. In summer, cut that year's new growth back to five buds from the main stem, to aid air circulation and fruiting.

On cordons, during summer reduce the length of the laterals off a main vertical stem to one bud from the previous year's cut. In early spring cut the main stem back by one-quarter of the previous year's growth. To prune a fan-trained plant, treat each stem as if it were a cordon.

HARVEST

The first haul of fruit for cooking and preserving should be ready in late spring or early summer. Take off about half of the fruits now, or as many as you need. Those that remain will be larger and sweeter by midsummer. Lift the end of the branch to reveal the hanging fruit – and the thorns – beneath. Be careful!

Use in:
- Gooseberry jam (page 41)
- Gooseberry cheese (page 42)

Gooseberry jam

The epitome of efficient kitchen gardening, this green gooseberry jam uses the first harvest of small fruits that are thinned from the branches to allow the rest to swell and ripen fully. It also happens to be delectable. Of course you can also use this recipe for later-season, ripe gooseberries, which will make a pink-tinged rather than green jam.

MAKES ABOUT 1.5KG/3LB 5OZ

INGREDIENTS
- 1kg/2lb 3oz gooseberries, topped and tailed
- 400ml/14fl oz water
- 1kg/2lb 3oz granulated sugar

METHOD
- Put the fruit into a large pan with the water. Simmer until the fruit is soft but still whole, then add the sugar.
- Stir to dissolve the sugar, then turn up the heat and boil rapidly until the setting point is reached (see Testing for a set, page 32).
- Scoop out the scum, then stand the jam for 5 minutes before stirring and potting it into warm, sterilized jars.

Something a little different

ELDERFLOWER
The first early-summer picking of gooseberries coincides with the elderflower harvest, and those heady blooms add a lovely sweetness and a very English flavour to the jam. How many flowers to use depends entirely on your taste: for the merest hint, 6–8 heads (six large or eight small to medium-sized heads) will be enough; for a stronger flavour use 12–14 heads. Check over the flowers for insects, then tie them in a jelly bag and add them to the pan with the fruit and water. Remove the bag before adding the sugar, squeezing out as much liquid as possible back into the pan.

Store in a cool, dry, dark place
Keeps for a year or more

Take off the tops (old flower heads) and tails (stalks) of your gooseberries: before (left) and after (right) being prepared.

Grow
- Gooseberries (page 40)
- Elderflower (page 166)

Gooseberry cheese

This cheese, though it could just as easily be sliced to accompany cold meats or a cheese board, is rather nice as a jammy take on the more usual gooseberry fool. Make the cheeses in small individual ramekins or moulds, then turn them out into a bowl to serve. Give your guests a jug of rich, thick pouring cream and, hey presto, an instant, no-fuss dessert perfect for early summer. Alternatively, pot into jars as usual. Use your first or second gooseberry harvest.

MAKES ABOUT 600G/1LB 5OZ

INGREDIENTS
- 1kg/2lb 3oz gooseberries, topped and tailed
- 150ml/¼ pint water
- granulated sugar (250g per 400ml/8oz per 14fl oz of pulp; see method)
- sunflower or other unflavoured oil

METHOD
- Put the gooseberries into a large pan with the water. Simmer gently over a low–medium heat, stirring often, until the fruit is soft.
- Push the entire contents of the pan through a sieve into a clean pan.
- Add the appropriate amount of sugar and stir until it has all dissolved.
- Over a medium heat, boil very gently until the mixture is reduced and thick. Stir often to stop it sticking to the base (take care – it will spit). The mixture is ready when you can part it, to leave a clean track on the base of the pan.
- Meanwhile brush the insides of clean, sterilized ramekins with a very thin layer of the oil.
- Pour the mixture into the ramekins and tap or stir to release any air bubbles in the corners. Cover with wax discs or oiled greaseproof paper cut to fit.
- Once cool, wrap the ramekins tightly in clingfilm and store until needed. Take them out an hour or so before serving.
- Alternatively, pot the hot mixture into warm, sterilized jars.

Grow
- Gooseberries (page 40)

Store Ramekins: in the refrigerator; Jars: in a cool, dry, dark place
Keeps Ramekins: for a month or more; Jars: for a year or more

Growing redcurrants

I love my currant bushes. I give them maybe five hours of attention over the whole year, and each provides me with up to 4kg/8lb 12oz of fruit every year and will continue to do so for the next twenty years, all for the price of a single, measly punnet of fruit from the supermarket. Oh, and the flowers and fruit are really pretty too.

BEST VARIETIES
'Stanza', 'Red Lake' and 'Jonkheer van Tets' all give reliably heavy harvests of redcurrants.

Whitecurrants, and the less widely available pinkcurrants, have exactly the same cultivation methods, although of course will not produce quite the same coloured preserves. But, if you want to give these a go too try 'Versailles Blanche' for a whitecurrant. Pinkcurrant variety choice is more likely to come down to whatever you can find.

PLANTING
Redcurrants crop well in partial shade, although not as heavily as in full sun (I used to grow mine successfully in a north-facing, heavily shaded garden). They tolerate most soils except waterlogged ones. Allow 1.2sq m/ 13sq ft for each bush, or grow as cordons or fans.

MAINTENANCE
Mulch with compost in early spring, and keep well-watered if the weather is dry as the fruit begins to swell. You may want to protect your crop with netting from the birds – red fruits are particularly attractive to them.

Prune bushes in early spring before the leaves appear, to create an open goblet framework of around ten branches. Cut back last year's new shoots to two buds from the main stem. In summer, cut that year's new growth back to five buds from the main stem, to aid air circulation and fruiting.

For cordons, in summer reduce the length of the laterals off a main vertical stem to one bud from the previous year's cut. In early spring, cut the main stem back by one-quarter of the previous year's growth. To prune a fan-trained plant, treat each stem as if it were a cordon.

HARVEST
Wait until all the berries are red (or a creamy white for whitecurrants) and then leave them for a few more days. Pick the entire strig (the name given to the pendulous stem of currants) off the main branch and then separate currants and strigs in the kitchen later.

Use in:
• Redcurrant jelly (page 46)
• Bar-le-duc (page 48)

Redcurrant jelly

This savoury jelly is both brilliantly coloured and brilliant. It is so versatile: use it with any roast meat, or stir a spoonful into a stew or tomato sauce. It is also really easy to make – because the whole redcurrant bunch will be strained through a jelly bag, there's no need to take the individual currants off the strig, or indeed tail them either.

MAKES ABOUT 600G/1LB 5OZ

INGREDIENTS
- 1kg/2lb 3oz redcurrants including their strigs (if you have already removed the strigs, just weigh out a few extra grams, to compensate for the lack of strigs)
- 100ml/3½fl oz water
- granulated sugar (75g per 100ml/2½oz per 3½fl oz of pulp; see method)

METHOD
- Put the berries and the water in a large pan. Simmer gently over a low–medium heat, stirring often, until the fruit is soft and releasing its juices.
- Mash the fruit, then put the entire contents of the pan into a jelly bag. Leave to strain for at least 3 hours, and preferably overnight. Then discard the contents of the bag.
- Measure the juice and put it into a clean pan with the appropriate amount of sugar. Stir over a low heat to dissolve the sugar, then turn up the heat and bring to the boil.
- Boil rapidly until the setting point is reached (see Testing for a set, page 32).
- Remove any scum and pot into warm, sterilized jars.

Something a little different

RASPBERRIES
For a sweeter jelly, use 500g/1lb 2oz raspberries and 500g/1lb 2oz currants.

Store in a cool, dry, dark place
Keeps for a year or more

Grow
- Redcurrants
  (page 44)
- Raspberries
  (page 52)

Bar-le-duc

Named after the French town from which it originates, this conserve is traditionally made with redcurrants, but in fact white-, pink- or blackcurrants could also be used. It is much easier to pick the entire strigs of currants off the branch, and then use a fork to run down each strig to break off the currants into a bowl once you're back in the kitchen. My dog loves currant de-strigging time, and will hang around waiting for the odd one that pings off on to the floor.

MAKES ABOUT 900G/2LB

INGREDIENTS
- 500g/1lb 2oz redcurrants, de-stalked (tails can be retained)
- 750g/1lb 10oz granulated sugar

METHOD
- If you have the time, prick each currant with a clean needle, because this helps it to remain plump.
- Put the currants into a large ceramic or glass bowl and stir through the sugar. Cover and leave at room temperature overnight (up to 24 hours).
- Transfer everything to a large pan and bring slowly to a gentle boil.
- Boil for 3 minutes then take the pan off the heat. Stand for half an hour, by which time a skin should have formed over the surface.
- Stir, then pot into warm, sterilized jars.

Grow
- Redcurrants (page 44)

Store in a cool, dry, dark place; once opened, keep in the refrigerator
Keeps for three months or more

Growing blackcurrants

Blackcurrants are the easiest to grow of all the soft fruits. They are low-maintenance, and their pruning is incredibly simple, although they do take up slightly more space than redcurrants (see page 44). The leaves are a by-product: steep two or three in a cup of boiling water for a delicious herbal tea, or use them to make a flavoured syrup (see page 164).

BEST VARIETIES

Most of the blackcurrant varieties for home and commercial growing have been bred by the Scottish Crop Research Institute, and their 'Ben' series are all worth planting. Of them, 'Ben Sarek' is the most compact variety, and 'Ben Connan' provides early ripening and resistance to most pests and diseases.

PLANTING

Blackcurrants prefer full sun, and tolerate most soils including even heavy clays prone to temporary waterlogging. They need plenty of nutrients, so dig in a lot of organic matter before planting. Allow at least 1.5sq m/16sq ft for each plant, but it is better to leave 2sq m/22sq ft, to give you space to squeeze round for picking. Compact 'Ben Sarek' needs only 1.2sq m/13sq ft for each plant. Blackcurrants can be planted in pots, but the container needs to be sizeable.

Plant bare-root or potted plants in the dormant season, making sure that you bury the crown of each plant (where the roots meet the shoots) around 5cm/2in below the soil surface. This will stimulate the production of more shoots from the base.

MAINTENANCE

Water well in dry periods, especially during flowering and fruiting. Netting the plant prevents the birds from eating your crop.

In late winter or early spring, before the leaves emerge, cut around one-third of the stems back to the ground, focusing on removing the 4Ds (see page 16), then any other older stems to make up the total. This renews the plant and stimulates growth. Give the plant a thick mulch of garden compost after doing this.

Repot container-grown plants every 2–3 years and, if possible, move them under cover during flowering and/ or fruiting to protect from frost and birds respectively.

HARVEST

Wait until the currants are all deep purple-black, and resist the temptation to pick them for another few days, because this extra ripening time will enhance their sweetness.

Use in:
- Blackcurrant jam (page 50)
- Berry cordials and syrups (page 64)

Blackcurrant jam

My husband's favourite jam, this is the one I make in the largest quantities every year. It gets used in all the usual jammy ways, but I particularly like to spread it in the middle of a chocolate cake. Make sure you've taken off any little bits of stalk, but there's no need to take off the dried flower ends.

MAKES ABOUT 2.4KG/5LB 4OZ

INGREDIENTS
- 1kg/2lb 3oz blackcurrants, de-stalked
- 600ml/1 pint water
- 1.5kg/3lb 5oz granulated sugar

METHOD
- Put the prepared fruit in a large pan with the water. Cook at a gentle simmer until the fruit is soft (easily squished against the side of the pan with the back of a spoon), but still holding its shape.
- Add the sugar and stir until it is all dissolved, then bring to the boil.
- Boil rapidly until it reaches the setting point (see Testing for a set, page 32).
- Remove from the heat and leave to stand for 5 minutes while you scoop out any scum. Pot into warm, sterilized jars.

Grow
- Blackcurrants (page 49)
- Apples (page 76)

Store in a cool, dry, dark place
Keeps for a year or more

Something a little different

APPLE
If you do not have quite enough blackcurrants, and there is a cooking apple in the fruit bowl, use the apple to stretch your harvest a little further. These two fruits have a natural affinity of flavours.
- Use 650g/1lb 7oz blackcurrants, and 350g/12oz peeled, cored and chopped cooking apple.
- Add the apple flesh to the blackcurrants and water.

Growing raspberries, blackberries and hybrid berries

Known collectively as cane fruits, raspberries and blackberries have been bred together and with other similar species to create a rainbow's worth of differently coloured and flavoured hybrid berries, whose cultivation methods vary very little.

BEST VARIETIES

The humble raspberry is split into summer- and autumn-fruiting types, with the summer further divided into early, mid- and late-season varieties. Plant at least a 1m/3ft row for one season to have enough fruit to preserve: 'Tulameen' (mid/late) is a favourite of mine, as is 'Joan J', and most of the 'Glen' cultivars are great as well. Of the autumn croppers, 'Autumn Bliss' is by far the most widely available.

Blackberries in cultivation such as 'Loch Tay' are often bred to reduce the vigour and lack the prickles that make them hard-won fruit in the wild. Of the hybrids, black raspberries (e.g. 'Jewel'), loganberries and tayberries such as 'Buckingham' are all great candidates for jam making too.

Use in:
• Raspberry jam (page 53)
• Berry refrigerator jam
(page 71) • Raspberry curd
(page 54) • Bramble jam
(page 72) • Redcurrant and
raspberry jelly (page 46)

PLANTING

Good-quality, deep soil with good drainage provides the optimum conditions for successful harvests and, while blackberries and hybrids tolerate some shade, all cane fruit crops best in full sun. Plant raspberry canes 35cm/14in apart along a row, and blackberries and hybrids 2.5m/8ft apart, or more for vigorous cultivars – check the labels. Tie each plant into wires, either on a fence or fastened between two posts, with the wires spaced 60cm/24in apart for raspberries and 45cm/18in apart for blackberries and hybrids. Larger plants such as blackberries can be trained over arches.

MAINTENANCE

Tie the developing canes to the wires to prevent them bending under the weight of fruit or breaking in the wind – secure raspberries vertically, and blackberries and hybrids horizontally, along the wires.

Give the canes a thick mulch in spring, and keep well-watered during dry spells, especially as the fruit develops. Netting crops – or growing them in a fruit cage – will protect the berries from birds.

Pruning cane fruit can be summarized by the dictum 'remove the canes that bore fruit this year'. This means summer-fruiting raspberries, blackberries and hybrids need their fruited canes cut off at the end of their cropping season, and the new growth (which will bear fruit the following year) spaced out and re-tied to the wires. Autumn raspberries fruit on new growth each year, so all the canes are cut back to the ground each winter. In all cases, also remove dead or diseased wood, and anything of less than pencil-thickness.

Suckers are often produced – dig these out in spring and plant as replacements or in new rows – the canes will need replacing every ten years or so.

HARVEST

Berries will easily separate from the plant when ready; raspberries pull off their central plugs, which hold them to the rest of the plant, while others retain them.

Raspberry jam

My eight-year-old niece Elle announced recently that she is engaged to blueberries, but married to raspberries. Aside from the potential bigamy, I think I agree with her. This simple, quick jam gives us both raspberries year-round.

MAKES ABOUT 1.6KG/3LB 8OZ

INGREDIENTS
- 1kg/2lb 3oz raspberries
- 1kg/2lb 3oz granulated sugar

METHOD
- Put the raspberries in a large pan and simmer gently over a low heat, stirring often, until the fruit is soft.
- If you prefer to remove most of the seeds, push the entire contents through a sieve at this stage back into the pan, but make sure that all the fruit pulp and juice is returned and only the pips remain in the sieve.
- Add the sugar and stir to dissolve, then turn up the heat.
- Boil rapidly until the setting point is reached (see Testing for a set, page 32), then remove from the heat and stand for 5 minutes.
- Remove any scum, then stir and pot into warm, sterilized jars.

Grow
- Raspberries, blackberries and hybrid berries (page 52)
- Mint (page 156)
- Rose pelargonium (page 167)

Store in a cool, dry, dark place
Keeps for a year or more

Something a little different

MINT
Stir in 2 tbsp finely chopped mint (peppermint) leaves before potting.

BLACK PEPPER
Stir in 1 tbsp freshly ground black pepper before potting.

ROSE PELARGONIUM
Add a handful of rose pelargonium leaves to the fruit as it simmers, then remove them before adding the sugar.

LOGANBERRIES OR OTHER HYBRID BERRIES
Substitute loganberries or other hybrid berries for the raspberries either in whole or in part. Loganberries make a particularly fine jam.

Raspberry curd

Raspberries are probably my favourite soft fruit to use for curd, but you could just as easily substitute them in whole or in part with blackberries or even ripe gooseberries. This berry version is slightly thinner than the lemon curd on page 102, but still perfectly spreadable on toast and crumpets.

MAKES ABOUT 600G/1LB 5OZ

INGREDIENTS
- 300g/10oz raspberries
- 1 lemon, juiced
- 4 eggs
- 85g/3oz unsalted butter
- 170g/6oz caster sugar

METHOD
- Put all the ingredients in a ceramic or glass bowl set over a saucepan of simmering water on a medium heat – the bowl should fit snugly over the saucepan but not touch the water itself.
- Use a whisk to beat the eggs, break up the fruit and mix all the ingredients together (flecks of unmelted butter are fine at this stage).
- Switch to a wooden spoon (metal implements can taint the taste) and stir continuously; this does not need to be vigorous once the butter has melted, it is simply to keep the mixture moving off the base of the bowl, otherwise the eggs may scramble. Stirring from side to side incorporates the ingredients faster and more effectively than going round and round.
- The curd is ready when it is thick and smooth and a track remains after you have drawn your finger through it on the back of the spoon (this can take 15 minutes or more). It will thicken further as it cools.
- Strain the curd through a sieve to remove all the raspberry pips, then pot into warm, sterilized jars.

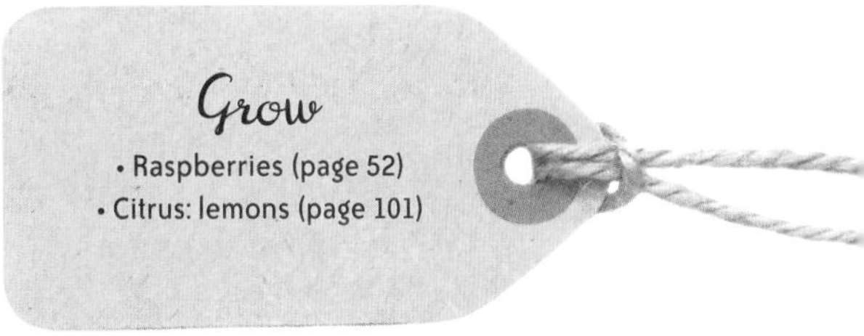

Grow
- Raspberries (page 52)
- Citrus: lemons (page 101)

Store in the refrigerator
Keeps for 3–4 weeks

Growing cherries

I grew up in Kent – the Garden of England – where orchards consisted largely of apple and cherry trees, and where growers often had market stalls in the high street specifically and solely to sell their cherry harvest. I'd buy two or more punnets at a time, for I knew I'd eat at least one punnet's worth on the way home.

BEST VARIETIES

Cherries are divided into sweet, acid (sour) and duke types, the last being a cross between the sweet and acid groups. Wild, or bird, cherries (*Prunus padus*) are a delicious hedgerow snack, but the stone-to-flesh ratio is poor and not ideal for jamming. Sweet varieties such as 'Stella' can be eaten fresh and are best for compote; 'May Duke' and the acid 'Morello' and 'Montmorency' are well-deserved classics for jam.

Check the rootstock and pollination group of your chosen cultivar ('Stella' and acid cherries are handily self-fertile). In cool-temperate areas, an acid cherry is likely to do better than a sweet variety, although the blossom will still be vulnerable to frost. There are some trees bred specifically for growing in pots or fruit cages – look for Cinderella or Ballerina on the label.

PLANTING

Plant bare-root or potted plants between autumn and late winter. Cherries flower early, so prefer the sunniest, warmest spot possible to offer the maximum protection to the blossom. A rich and well-drained soil is ideal so prepare the ground well. Trees can be trained as fans on south-facing walls, and those on dwarfing rootstocks are suitable for large pots.

MAINTENANCE

Trained and dwarf trees are the easiest to protect with netting from birds, which delight in taking your harvest in front of your eyes. An annual mulch with compost as well as always watering during dry weather, especially when each tree is flowering and fruiting, are all that is needed, apart from pruning. Do this in summer after the harvest, a tactic that helps to prevent the spread of a couple of specific cherry diseases. Aim to create an open goblet shape in free-standing trees, removing the 4Ds (see page 16) and any further stems required to maintain a good structure, but leaving plenty of wood that is at least one year old, for this is where the fruit is borne. Prune fan-trained trees to create and maintain their fan shapes, tying in replacement stems where necessary and shortening and thinning out laterals to keep growth in check while still retaining plenty of fruiting wood.

HARVEST

Pick once the fruit is a deep red (or black, depending on the cultivar) colour, and soft and sweet.

Use in:
- Cherry compote (page 59)
- Cherry jam (page 58)
- Berry cordials and syrups (page 64)

Cherry jam

It's really worth investing in a cherry pitter for this jam. If you don't have one, you can crush the fruit with a potato masher and then scoop out the stones as they float to the surface in the cooking jam, but there are always some that will escape your eagle eye and add a surprise crunch to your morning toast. Use acid or duke cherries for this jam, which has a deliciously tart, fabulous cherry flavour.

MAKES ABOUT 1.1KG/2LB 6OZ

INGREDIENTS
- 1kg/2lb 3oz acid cherries, pitted
- 3 lemons, halved and juiced
- 750g/1lb 10oz granulated sugar

METHOD
- Put the pitted cherries and lemon juice into a large pan, and place the cherry stones and the squeezed-out lemon halves into a jelly bag. Tie up the bag and add it to the pan.
- Simmer the fruit very gently over a low heat, stirring often, until the cherries are really soft. Remove the bag, squeezing out as much juice as possible back into the pan (wear rubber gloves to protect your hands).
- Add the sugar and stir until it is dissolved, then turn up the heat and bring to a boil.
- Boil rapidly until the jam reaches setting point (see Testing for a set, page 32), then remove it from the heat.
- Leave it to stand for 10 minutes while you remove any scum, then stir and pot into warm, sterilized jars.

Grow
- Cherries (page 56)
- Citrus: lemons (page 101)

Store in a cool, dry, dark place
Keeps for a year or more

Something a little different

VANILLA
I know it is highly unlikely that you are growing your own vanilla, but as you may have realized from other recipes in this book I quite like using desserts and puddings as inspiration for jam flavourings. Here the idea comes from clafoutis and cherry pie, and this variation adds just a background of vanilla and a little extra sweetness. Simply halve a vanilla pod lengthways and add it to the jelly bag.

Cherry compote

Fresh sweet cherries are such a treat that it seems a crime to preserve them. However I'm not above using them in desserts, and this compote is the ultimate in quick, seasonal puddings. It makes about enough for four servings. Just add mascarpone or vanilla ice cream – chocolate brownies optional. If there is any left over (unlikely), it keeps for a couple of days and is delicious with granola and yogurt.

MAKES ABOUT 400G/14OZ

INGREDIENTS
- 500g/1lb 2oz cherries, pitted
- 50g/2oz light muscovado sugar
- dash of kirsch, amaretto or brandy (optional)

METHOD
- Put the cherries, sugar and alcohol, if using, into a medium-sized pan. Swirl the pan to coat the cherries, then bring to the boil slowly.
- Lower the heat and simmer, stirring often, until the juices are reduced and sticky.
- Serve warm, or pot into warm, sterilized jars.

Grow
- Cherries (page 56)

Store in the refrigerator
Keeps for 2–3 days

Growing blueberries

Widely touted as a 'superfood' for its antioxidant properties, the blueberry is available year-round in supermarkets but is often rather insipid. If you have space for a large pot, you can grow your own blueberries and discover the variety and intensity of flavour offered by the domestic cultivars.

BEST VARIETIES
'Herbert' and 'Spartan' both have a great flavour. Blueberry bushes are partially self-fertile. If you have space for only one bush, you will still get fruit, but two or three bushes will produce significantly larger harvests from each plant.

PLANTING
Blueberries produce their best harvests when grown in full sun but also tolerate partial shade. They need free-draining, lime-free soil with a pH of 4–5.5, so it is generally preferable to grow them in containers or a specific raised bed, where the soil can be made sufficiently acidic or else use ericaceous compost and mix in some grit to aid drainage. In open ground allow 1.5sq m/16sq ft between plants.

MAINTENANCE
Water frequently, using rainwater to avoid raising the soil pH with alkaline tap water. Apply a controlled-release fertilizer and a mulch of compost in spring.

Pruning is as simple as cutting one or two older branches back to the ground during the dormant season (and removing the 4Ds at the same time; see page 16).

HARVEST
Depending on the variety, blueberries can be picked from late summer to early autumn. The berries are ready when fully coloured, soft and sweet – pull them gently off each bush.

Use in:
- Blueberry conserve (page 62)
- Berry cordials and syrups (page 64)

Blueberry conserve

Cooking blueberries really brings out their flavours and superb deep blue colour, but for a conserve you do this for a shorter time than for a jam. Blueberries also lend themselves very well to floral and lemon flavours, as in the variations in the box, below.

MAKES ABOUT 600G/1LB 5OZ

INGREDIENTS

- 450g/1lb blueberries, de-stalked
- 450g/1lb granulated sugar
- 1 lemon, juiced
- pinch of fine sea salt

METHOD

- Put the fruit in a large ceramic or glass bowl, then add 225g/8oz of the sugar, the lemon juice and salt. Stir everything together well.
- Cover and leave to stand at room temperature overnight (up to 24 hours). Stir the mixture whenever you remember (putting the bowl near the kettle helps!).
- Tip the contents of the bowl into a large pan and warm it over a low heat, stirring constantly.
- Once the mixture is warm, add the rest of the sugar and keep stirring until it is all dissolved.
- Turn up the heat and bring to a boil, then boil rapidly until it reaches the setting point (see Testing for a set, page 32).
- Take the pan off the heat and stand for 5 minutes (remove any scum) before stirring and potting into warm, sterilized jars.

Something a little different

LAVENDER

Add ½ tsp lavender (*Lavandula*) flowers to the fruit in the bowl. Alternatively use lavender-scented sugar in place of plain granulated.

LEMON VERBENA

Lemon verbena (*Aloysia citrodora*) gives a little citrus lift to the conserve. Add ½ tsp finely chopped fresh leaves to the fruit in the bowl, or replace the plain granulated sugar with lemon verbena-scented sugar.

Store in a cool, dry, dark place; once opened, keep in the refrigerator
Keeps for three months or more

Berry cordials and syrups

Berries are the most popular versions of these liquids in my house, either as single fruits or a mixture of whatever odds and ends we have, but we also use cherries, plums or rhubarb. Make a batch with whatever is in season when the previous batch runs out! Dilute the cordial with water – or add a dash to cocktails – for a fruity drink, and use syrups to drizzle over ice cream, pavlova or other puddings.

MAKES ABOUT 1 LITRE/1¾ PINTS CORDIAL; ABOUT 650ML/1 PINT SYRUP

INGREDIENTS
- 1.25kg/2lb 12oz fruit (any de-stalked or hulled berries or currants or a mixture)
- granulated sugar (50g per 100ml/2oz per 3½fl oz of pulp; see method)

METHOD: CORDIAL
- Roughly chop any large fruits so all the pieces are the same size.
- Put the fruit into a large pan with just enough water to cover the base. Simmer gently over a low heat until the fruit is soft and broken down, then mash with a potato masher.
- Pour the entire contents into a jelly bag. Leave it to run until the steady stream slows to a drip, then squeeze gently to get a stream going again. Once this begins to falter, discard the contents of the bag.
- Measure the juice and put into a clean pan with the appropriate amount of sugar. Put the pan over a low heat and stir to dissolve the sugar, then bring to the boil.
- Once the liquid is boiling, pour it into warm, sterilized bottles and seal.

METHOD: SYRUP
- Follow the method as for cordial until the liquid is boiling. Then reduce the heat so the liquid simmers very slowly and cook until it is reduced and syrupy (it will thicken further as it cools).
- Pour into warm, sterilized bottles and seal.

Grow
- Strawberries (page 36) • Raspberries, blackberries and hybrid berries (page 52) • Redcurrants (page 44)
- Blackcurrants (page 49)
- Blueberries (page 60)

Store in a cool, dry, dark place; once opened, keep in the refrigerator
Keeps for three months or more

Growing plums, gages, damsons and apricots

Although plums are ever popular as a fresh fruit, gages (greengages), apricots and damsons are harder to come by, so it really is worth having a tree or two if you have space. These fruit trees are all closely related, so look after them in the same way.

BEST VARIETIES

Plum varieties are split into cooking and eating types; the cookers are better for jams and jellies. They are further divided into those varieties with stones that will part easily from the flesh (a trait much valued after pitting 1kg/2lb 3oz or more of fruit) and those that do not (stick-stones). If you are buying several trees, make sure they are in compatible pollination groups (see page 14), or choose self-fertile varieties. Later-flowering varieties are also better for cool-temperate areas where the blossom may be destroyed by frost.

Good choices for plums include 'Stanley' and 'Marjorie's Seedling' and for greengages 'Cambridge Gage' or 'Oullins Gage'. Try Flavorcot ('Bayoto') or 'Moorpark' for apricots (all self-fertile) – later fruiting varieties that have a better chance against the frosts at blossom time. Damson variety names tend to be less consistent and there are fewer available, but 'Farleigh Damson' and 'Prune Damson' (also known as 'Shropshire Prune') are both good.

PLANTING

Plums, gages and damsons all prefer a sunny site with shelter from winds, and are ideal for training against a sunny wall or fence (a fan shape is the traditional form, but they can also be grown in cordons). They are tolerant of most soils provided they do not get waterlogged. Plant bare-root trees in autumn or late winter, and potted trees in autumn or spring, allowing around 2.5m/8ft between trees, 4m/13ft between fans and 75cm/2½ft between cordons. Stake each one or tie it to wires.

All plum, gage and damson trees on dwarfing rootstocks can be grown in large pots too. It is also possible to buy miniature cordoned trees, sometimes known as Ballerina or Cinderella trees, which have been specifically bred for patio pots. However the variety choice for these dwarf types is much smaller.

Apricots are fully hardy, but their early blossom is most likely to be damaged by frosts in temperate climates, so plant in the sunniest, warmest spot you have (a south-facing wall preferably) or in a large pot that can be protected in a greenhouse during late winter and early spring.

MAINTENANCE

Apply a mulch of organic matter in spring. Prune bush trees in spring and fan- and cordon-trained trees in summer (see Trained forms, page 15). Unlike other tree fruit, plums and their kin are pruned when in leaf to avoid spreading a couple of diseases specific to this family. Make sure no fruit is left rotting on the tree, to also help minimize the spread of disease.

HARVEST

Depending on the variety, plums, gages and apricots will ripen from midsummer to autumn, and damsons in autumn. If the weather or wasps are moving in, unripe fruit can be picked to mature indoors, but if possible leave it on the tree until the merest nudge knocks it off the branch.

Use in:

- Damson jelly (page 94)
- Greengage jam (page 68)
- High Dumpsideary jam (page 75) • Mincemeat (page 89) • Plum ketchup (page 70)
- Berry cordials and syrups (page 64)

Greengage jam

Greengage jam is pretty hard to find in the shops, and plum jam hardly less so. This is a real shame, because they are both delicious, very easy to make and a great use for a glut of fruit.

INGREDIENTS
- 1kg/2lb 3oz greengages, pitted
- 1 lemon, zest and juice
- 1kg/2lb 3oz granulated sugar

METHOD
- Put the greengage stones into a jelly bag. Roughly chop the flesh (you do not want any large pieces of skin to persist in the final jam) and put into a large pan.
- Add the lemon zest to the fruit. Put the squeezed lemon halves into the jelly bag, tie it up and put it in the pan.
- Add cold water to the lemon juice to bring it to a total volume of 200ml/7fl oz, then add this liquid to the pan.
- Cook gently over a medium heat until the fruit is very soft, then remove the jelly bag, squeezing as much liquid back into the pan as possible (wear rubber gloves to protect your hands).
- Mash the fruit gently to break up any remaining large, lumpy bits.
- Add the sugar and stir until it is completely dissolved, then turn up the heat and bring the jam to a boil.
- Boil rapidly until the jam reaches setting point (see Testing for a set, page 32), skim off any scum, then pot into warm, sterilized jars.

Something a little different

PLUM
Substitute plums for the greengages, and omit the lemon.

APRICOT
It is worth making your own apricot jam if you also cook a lot of cakes and patisserie. Simply substitute apricots for the greengages.

AMARETTO
Almonds are from the same botanical family as plums and gages, and thus amaretto really enhances their flavour.
- Stir in a dash (to taste) to the jam just before potting.

Grow
- Plums, gages, damsons and apricots (page 66)
- Citrus: lemons (page 101)

Store in a cool, dry, dark place
Keeps for a year or more

Plum ketchup

Plums' tart sweetness lends itself well to a ketchup such as this. The ginger and garlic flavourings make it an ideal accompaniment to anything that would traditionally be served with plum sauce: try it with shredded duck meat and lettuce in a brioche bun.

MAKES ABOUT 500ML/17½FL OZ

INGREDIENTS
- 1 shallot, halved lengthways
- 3 garlic cloves, unpeeled
- knob of fresh ginger root (8cm/3in long), unpeeled
- 1.5kg/3lb 5oz plums, halved and pitted
- 1 lemon, juiced
- 1 tbsp soy sauce
- 100g/3½oz light muscovado sugar
- salt and pepper, to taste

METHOD
- Preheat the oven to 180°C/350°F/gas mark 4.
- Unfurl the shallot layers and spread them and the garlic cloves over the base of a baking dish. Roughly chop the ginger and add to the dish.
- Add the plum halves to the dish in a layer over the shallot, garlic and ginger. Bake for 45 minutes, then remove from the oven and leave to sit for 15 minutes.
- Push the contents of the baking dish through a sieve into a large saucepan, leaving behind only the skins.
- Add the lemon juice and soy sauce to the purée and bring to a simmer over a medium heat.
- Once simmering, add the sugar and stir to dissolve, then continue to simmer until the ketchup is thickened and reduced, stirring regularly (30–40 minutes). It should be pourable, but a little on a spoon will plop off rather than run off.
- Season with salt and pepper, then pour into warm, sterilized bottles and seal.

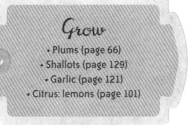

Grow
- Plums (page 66)
- Shallots (page 129)
- Garlic (page 121)
- Citrus: lemons (page 101)

Store in a cool, dry, dark place; once opened, leave in the refrigerator
Keeps for three months or more; once open lasts for a month or more

Berry refrigerator jam

Refrigerator jam is exactly what it says on the jar – it relies on the chilling of the refrigerator for part of its set and preservation, and therefore contains less sugar. It doesn't keep as long as more conventional jam, so the quantities are deliberately low here. I like to make some refrigerator jam for immediate use, then some other jam to see me through the winter. Though raspberries and strawberries work best, you can also make refrigerator jam with blackberries or hybrid berries.

MAKES ABOUT 550G/1LB 4OZ

INGREDIENTS
- 500g/1lb 2oz hulled strawberries, raspberries, blackberries or hybrid berries
- 250g/8oz jam sugar

METHOD
- Cut any large berries (that is, large strawberries) in half or quarters so all the fruit is approximately the same size. Put about half into a large pan and crush it roughly with a potato masher, then add the rest of the fruit.
- Warm the fruit slowly over a low–medium heat. As soon as it reaches a simmer, add the sugar and stir until it is dissolved.
- Bring to the boil and boil rapidly for 5 minutes (7 minutes for strawberries).
- Remove the pan from the heat and leave it to stand for 5 minutes, then pot into warm, sterilized jars.
- Once the jars have cooled to room temperature, put them into the refrigerator.

Grow
- Raspberries, blackberries and hybrid berries (page 52)
- Strawberries (page 36)

Store in the refrigerator
Keeps for a month or more if unopened; once open, lasts for only a month

Bramble jam

I used to make bramble jelly with my blackberries, but to my greedy eyes the final volume of jelly always seemed a poor return on the time spent picking and the weight of fruit. This robust, scrumptious jam that celebrates the late-summer harvest and heralds the onset of autumn, and also happens to be my favourite crumble filling, is the answer.

Something a little different

BAY
Blackberries and bay (*Laurus nobilis*) are a great combination.
- Add 6 bay leaves to the fruit when it goes into the pan.
- Remove the bay leaves before adding the sugar.

Grow
- Blackberries (page 52)
- Apples (page 76)
- Bay (page 154)

MAKES ABOUT 1.2KG/2LB 10OZ

INGREDIENTS
- 250g/8oz peeled, cored and diced cooking apples
- 500g/1lb 2oz blackberries
- 150ml/¼ pint water
- 750g/1lb 10oz granulated sugar

METHOD
- Add the diced apples to the pan with the blackberries and the water and cook very gently over a low heat until the fruit is soft.
- Crush it together with a potato masher, then stir in the sugar until it is dissolved.
- Turn up the heat and bring the jam to a boil, then boil rapidly until it reaches setting point (see Testing for a set, page 32).
- Scoop off any scum and pot into warm, sterilized jars.

Store in a cool, dry, dark place
Keeps for a year or more

LATE SUMMER AND AUTUMN

High Dumpsideary jam

One of those recipes that is steeped in folklore, legend has it this jam was created by a Mr Dumpsideary (or Dumpsidearie) when his wife wanted jam and all they had were a few windfalls and some spices. Whatever the origins, it is a useful one if you have only a little of each fruit. Traditionally the recipe also includes cloves, but I think the hint of cinnamon by itself is just enough to signal the approach of autumn. The jelly bag needs to be nestled in the fruit for the whole time it is in the pan. You may therefore need to use two pans: a deep, smaller one to cook the fruit initially, and a large one once you have added the sugar.

MAKES ABOUT 900G/2LB

INGREDIENTS

- 300g/10oz plums, halved and pitted
- 300g/10oz pears, peeled, cored and chopped
- 300g/10oz cooking apples, peeled, cored and sliced
- 1 lemon, juiced
- 1 cinnamon stick
- 100ml/3½fl oz water
- 780g/1lb 12oz granulated sugar

METHOD

- Put the plum stones into a jelly bag.
- Place the plums, pears and apples in a deep pan. Add the lemon juice to the fruit in the pan and the lemon halves to the jelly bag with the cinnamon stick. Tie up the bag and put it in with the fruit.
- Add the water to the pan and cook, covering it and stirring regularly, over a low heat until the fruit is soft and pulpy (squash any larger bits against the side of the pan with the back of a spoon).
- Remove the jelly bag and squeeze the liquid out of it back into the pan. Discard the bag's contents.
- Add the sugar to the fruit and stir to dissolve, then bring to the boil.
- Boil rapidly until a setting point is reached (see Testing for a set, page 32).
- Remove any scum and pot into warm, sterilized jars.

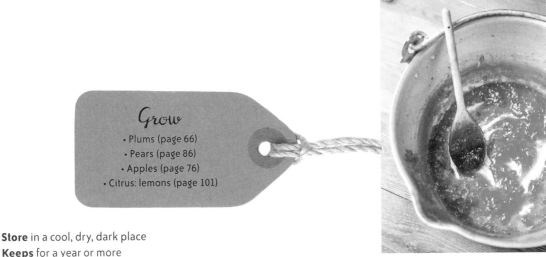

Grow
- Plums (page 66)
- Pears (page 86)
- Apples (page 76)
- Citrus: lemons (page 101)

Store in a cool, dry, dark place
Keeps for a year or more

Growing apples

Having a garden large enough to establish an orchard has been one of my long-held dreams. The joy of fresh apples, straight from the tree, and the sheer abundance of fruit cannot compare with buying from even the best farmers' market. Until that day I will continue to grow my fruit trees in large pots, because lack of space is really not an obstacle when it comes to fruit growing, especially apples, which can be trained in so many ways.

BEST VARIETIES

Both cooking and dessert apples lend themselves to preserving, depending on the recipe. Cooking apples will break down to a mush, while dessert apples hold their form for longer and tend to be sweeter to start with. Check the rootstocks (see page 14) and pollination groups (see page 14) or plant a crab apple as well to aid pollination.

Cooking varieties include the classic 'Bramley's Seedling', or try 'Blenheim Orange', which is a good cooking and dessert variety. There are hundreds of dessert apple cultivars and you might like to plant local heritage trees, but my favourites include 'Cox's Orange Pippin', 'Orleans Reinette', 'Ashmead's Kernel' and 'Egremont Russet'.

PLANTING

Apple trees still perform in partial shade but will do better in a sunny site with good air circulation. Plant bare-root trees in the dormant season, and potted trees in autumn or spring. Apples tolerate most soils and situations except boggy ones. Stake or tie to wires for free-standing or trained trees respectively (see page 15).

MAINTENANCE

Prune free-standing apples between leaf fall and bud burst, and cut back trained trees in summer and then winter as required (see page 16). Mulch with well-rotted organic matter and some controlled-release fertilizer in spring. Water during dry spells, especially during flowering and fruiting. In midsummer, thin the fruit by removing all but the two or three biggest from each cluster, although the tree will do much of this itself in early summer. Trained trees especially benefit from the fruit being thinned.

HARVEST

Harvest from late summer to late autumn, depending on the variety. Windfalls will give an indication that the fruit is ripening; apples are ready when the stalk breaks easily from the branch as the fruit is lifted.

CRAB APPLES

Crab apple trees are great for small gardens, producing an abundance of blossom and then fruit that is perfect for preserving. They are better grown free-standing rather than trained. They need minimal pruning – only to remove the 4Ds (see page 16) – and are otherwise cared for just as cooking and dessert apple trees (see above). Good varieties include 'Golden Hornet', 'Profusion' and 'John Downie'.

Use in:

- Apple chutney (page 82)
- Windfall marmalade (page 78)
- Apple pie curd (page 80)
- Black butter (page 84)
- Mostarda di frutta (page 88)
- Mincemeat (page 89)
- Blackcurrant jam (page 50)
- Bramble jam (page 72)

Windfall marmalade

Marmalade ingredients need not be restricted to oranges, and this alternative is a brilliant way to avoid wasting windfall apples. Red grapefruits give this marmalade a traditional colour and provide the shredded peel. As the windfall apples are likely to have large bruises, take out any bad bits before weighing them.

MAKES ABOUT 1.3KG/2LB 14OZ

INGREDIENTS
- 2 red grapefruit
- 500g/1lb 2oz windfall apples (cooking or dessert), peeled, cored and sliced
- 1.5 litres/3 pints water
- 1.1kg/2lb 6oz granulated sugar

METHOD
- Using a potato peeler, pare the peel from the grapefruit and shred it finely into short lengths. Cut the flesh away from the pith. Put the pith into a jelly bag, and chop the flesh into small pieces, removing any membranes while doing so to prevent them persisting as lumps in the final marmalade.
- Add the apple peel and cores into the jelly bag, and place the apple slices and shredded grapefruit peel and flesh in a pan.
- Tie up the jelly bag and add it to the pan with the water.
- Bring to the boil, then reduce the heat and simmer, uncovered, for around 2 hours until the peel is soft and the contents reduced by half.
- Wearing rubber gloves to protect your hands, remove the jelly bag and squeeze as much liquid as possible back into the pan. Discard the contents of the bag.
- Add the sugar to the pan and stir until it dissolves, then bring the marmalade to the boil. Boil rapidly until the setting point is reached (see Testing for a set, page 32).
- Remove the pan from the heat and leave to stand for 10 minutes, to ensure that the peel will be well-distributed through each jar. Stir the marmalade, then pot it into warm, sterilized jars.

Grow
- Apples (page 76)
- Citrus: grapefruit (page 101)

Store in a cool, dry, dark place
Keeps for a year or more

Apple pie curd

There is of course no actual pie in this apple pie curd, but it tastes just like cooked apples and custard. Serve it in little pastry cases for a quick and easy 'apple pie', or use it as you would any other curd or spread. I have not given it a dedicated variation below, but, if you like cinnamon in your apple pie, add some to taste before potting.

MAKES 350G/12OZ

INGREDIENTS
- 1 large cooking apple (300–350g/10–12oz), peeled, cored and roughly chopped
- ½ lemon, juiced
- 2 eggs
- 50g/2oz unsalted butter, cubed
- 100g/3½oz caster sugar

METHOD
- Put the apple flesh and peel into a small pan with a splash of water (just enough to stop the apple sticking to the base). Cook very gently and uncovered over a low–medium heat, stirring often until the apple flesh is soft and pulpy. Rub the contents through a sieve into a large ceramic or glass bowl. Discard the peel left in the sieve.
- Add the lemon juice, eggs, butter and sugar to the bowl. Then fit the bowl over a pan of simmering water on a medium heat – the bowl should sit snugly over the pan but not touch the water itself.
- Use a whisk to incorporate all the ingredients (flecks of unmelted butter are fine at this stage). Then switch to a wooden spoon (metal implements can taint the taste) and stir continuously for 10–15 minutes to keep the mixture moving off the base of the bowl and thereby prevent the eggs from scrambling.
- The curd is ready when it coats the back of the spoon and a track remains when you draw your finger through it. Leave it to thicken further as it cools.
- Pot into warm, sterilized jars.

Something a little different

APPLE AND BLACKBERRY PIE CURD
- Use a smaller (250–300g/8–10oz) apple and add 50–75g/2–2½oz blackberries to the apple flesh and peel.
- To catch any blackberry seeds that may have snuck through during the first sieving, re-sieve the cooked curd before potting.

APPLE AND QUINCE PIE CURD
This variation was suggested by my friend Alison who lives, appropriately, in a cottage called 'Bramleys'.
- Use a 150–175g/5–6oz apple and a 150–175g/5–6oz quince.
- Wash the fluff off the quince skin before peeling and coring it. Chop the quince flesh very finely so that it will cook in the same time as the apple.
- Add only the quince flesh to the pan at the same time as the apple flesh and peel.

Store in the refrigerator
Keeps for about a month

Apple chutney

This classic autumn chutney is excellent with cheese and pork in particular. The dessert apples and walnuts give it a bit of bite, and there is just a hint of sage. If you prefer a stronger flavour, add more sage to taste.

MAKES ABOUT 1.5KG/3LB 5OZ

INGREDIENTS

- 375g/13oz red onions, finely chopped
- 675g/1½lb cooking apples, peeled, cored and finely sliced
- 225g/8oz dessert apples, peeled, cored and finely sliced
- 200g/7oz sultanas
- 300ml/½ pint cider vinegar
- 100ml/3½fl oz water
- 300g/10oz demerara sugar
- 1 tsp salt
- 3 tbsp finely chopped sage leaves (optional)
- 100g/3½oz walnuts, roughly chopped (optional)

METHOD

- Put the onion pieces into a large pan. Add the apple flesh to the pan, together with all the other ingredients.
- Over a low–medium heat, stir everything together well to incorporate the ingredients and dissolve the sugar.
- Cook at a very gentle simmer, uncovered, for around 2 hours or until the chutney can be parted cleanly on the base of the pan. Stir it regularly during this time.
- Pot into warm, sterilized jars and leave to mature for a month before eating.

Grow
- Apples (page 76)
- Onions (page 129)
- Sage (page 157)

Store in a cool, dry, dark place; once opened, keep in the refrigerator
Keeps for a year or more

Black butter

Black butter, or *nièr beurre*, is a traditional recipe from Jersey. Although the recipe itself is a closely guarded secret, the ingredients list on the jar I bought gives enough clues – this is my version which comes pretty close to their original. Being dark and treacly, it's the Heathcliff or Darcy of the jam world, all brooding and intense. Try black butter in mince pies as an alternative to Mincemeat (page 89), or spoon it over vanilla ice cream.

Something a little different

WITH APPLE BRANDY
For a little alcoholic hit, add a dash of apple brandy when you stir in the treacle and spices.

MAKES ABOUT 1.35KG/3LB

INGREDIENTS
- 1.2 litres/2 pints cider (sweet or medium)
- 1.5kg/3lb 5oz dessert apples, peeled, cored and finely sliced
- 2 lemons, zest and juice
- granulated sugar (50g/2oz per 100ml/3½fl oz of pulp; see method)
- 100g/3½oz black treacle
- 15g/½oz liquorice, very finely diced
- 1 tsp mixed spice
- 1 tsp ground cinnamon

METHOD
- Pour the cider into a large pan and bring to the boil. Continue boiling until the volume is reduced to 600ml/1 pint.
- Meanwhile prepare the apple slices, tossing them in the lemon juice as you do so, to help prevent them from browning.
- Add the apple slices, lemon zest and juice to the reduced cider and cook gently, stirring regularly, until the contents are soft, pulpy and reduced.
- (I rather like the odd chunk of apple flesh in the final butter, as it gives it a bit of bite, but if you prefer a smooth consistency blend the contents to a smooth purée at this point.)
- Measure the pulp, and weigh out the appropriate amount of sugar.
- Return the pulp and sugar to a clean pan and add the rest of the ingredients. Simmer gently over a low heat, stirring frequently to prevent the mixture sticking to the base of the pan, but watch out as it can spit. Remove from the heat once the mixture is thick and there is no free liquid.
- Pot at once into warm, sterilized jars.

Store in a cool, dry, dark place
Keeps for a year or more

Grow
- Apples (page 76)
- Citrus: lemons (page 101)

Growing pears

Pear trees can look a little weedy next to apple trees in an orchard setting – they are generally smaller and narrower – but in trained form the blossom and fruit are easier to admire. It will be a few years until your trees bear fruit but once they are mature, and with very little input, you will have pears to eat, preserve and give away every year.

BEST VARIETIES

As with all tree fruit, it is important to make sure you choose varieties from the right pollination groups and on a suitable rootstock for your situation (see page 14). Pears are split into cooking and dessert varieties, but either is suitable for preserving. Dessert 'Conference' is reliable and has a good flavour (explaining why it is so widely available), while dessert pear 'Doyenné du Comice' is more temperamental, but the taste is worth the extra trouble. The cooker 'Black Worcester' is also a good choice.

PLANTING

Plant bare-root trees in the dormant season, and potted trees in autumn or spring. At the same time attach training wires (if appropriate), and stake free-standing trees. Pears blossom early in the season and their flowers can be damaged by spring winds and frosts, so plant in a sheltered, warm spot.

Pears can also be grown in large pots, but be sure to choose a tree on a dwarfing rootstock.

MAINTENANCE

Water in dry spells, especially once the tree is flowering and then producing fruit. Remove most of the fruitlets in late spring or early summer in any large clusters to allow decent-sized pears to develop. Prune annually, in summer (for trained trees) or winter (for free-standing ones), see page 16.

HARVEST

Pears are ready to harvest when the stalk breaks naturally from the branch when each fruit is gently lifted. Depending on the variety this can be from late summer to mid-autumn. The flesh will still be hard, and cookers will be a bit gritty, but should taste sweet. Pears will then need a little ripening indoors and will be ready to eat when soft to a gentle squeeze near the stalk.

Use in:
- Pear caramel (page 90)
- Pâté de fruit (page 100)
- Mostarda di frutta (page 88)

Mostarda di frutta

This Italian relish is also known as mostarda di Cremona. *The Silver Spoon*, that bible of Italian cookery, defines mostarda di frutta as 'an Italian speciality of candied fruit immersed in a syrup of honey, mustard and wine. It may be mild or strong and is eaten with roasted and boiled meat and sharp cheeses . . . for salad dressings and flavouring stews'.

Note: Using plums and red grapes will colour the sugar syrup pink.

Grow
- Apples (page 76)
- Pears (page 86)
- Quinces (page 96)
- Plums, gages, damsons and apricots (page 66)
- Grapes (page 92)

Store in a cool, dry, dark place; once opened, keep in the refrigerator
Keeps for six months or more; once opened lasts for a month

MAKES ABOUT 1.2KG/2LB 10OZ

INGREDIENTS
- 1.3kg/2lb 14oz autumn fruits (dessert apples, pears, quinces, plums/greengages/apricots, grapes – a mixture of some or all of these is best)
- 300ml/½ pint white wine vinegar
- 450g/1lb granulated sugar
- 200g/7oz honey
- 300ml/½ pint water
- 7 tbsp mustard powder
- 1 tsp salt

METHOD
- Prepare the fruit: peel and core any apples, pears and quinces, and cut into quarters or sixths; halve and pit any plums, greengages and apricots; and remove each grape from its stalk.
- Put the vinegar, sugar, honey and water into a large pan and slowly bring to the boil, stirring to dissolve the sugar and honey. Scoop out any scum from the syrup during this process.
- Keeping the syrup at a steady simmer, cook the fruit in batches, turning it often and carefully in the syrup. Do the pale-coloured fruits first, and cook each fruit type until just tender – the quinces will take the longest time to soften, followed by the apples, the pears, the plums/greengages/apricots and finally the grapes. Once each batch is cooked, remove it from the pan with a slotted spoon and put into a large ceramic or glass bowl.
- After the final batch of fruit has been removed from the pan, pour the syrup over the fruit in the bowl, cover and leave at room temperature for 24 hours.
- Drain the syrup into a pan and bring to a simmer. Add all the fruit and bring to the boil, then remove from the heat.
- Scoop out the fruit and transfer it to a warm, sterilized jar (a large Kilner jar is ideal), arranging the different fruit types in layers, yet making sure that the grapes are not the final layer as they will float.
- Stir the mustard powder and salt into the syrup until they have dissolved, then return the pan to the heat. Once the syrup is boiling, pour it into the jar until the fruit is completely submerged but there is still clear space beneath the rim.
- Seal, and leave to mature for at least 2 weeks.

Mincemeat

Home-made mincemeat is so much better than shop-bought that it does not stand real comparison. By potting up this fruity, virtually fat-free version in autumn (and making and freezing some pastry), you can really get ahead for Christmas. A spoonful or two in an apple pie or crumble is also delicious, if you have any mincemeat left over. This is my version of Pam Corbin's recipe in *The River Cottage Preserves Handbook*.

MAKES ABOUT 2KG/4LB 7OZ

INGREDIENTS
- 2 large oranges, zest and juice
- 250g/8oz damsons
- 750g/1lb 10oz plums, halved and pitted
- 500g/1lb 2oz dessert apples, peeled, cored and diced into 1cm/½in cubes
- 600g/1lb 5oz sultanas
- 100g/3½oz marmalade
- 250g/8oz demerara sugar
- ½ tsp ground cloves
- 2 tsp ground ginger
- ½ nutmeg, finely grated
- 100g/3½oz almonds, chopped
- 3 tbsp amaretto

METHOD
- Put the orange juice into a large pan with the whole damsons and prepared plums. Cook gently until the fruit is tender.
- Put the apple cubes, sultanas, marmalade, sugar, spices, almonds and the orange zest into a large baking dish and stir well.
- Rub the contents of the damson/plum mixture through a sieve to form a purée. Do this in batches and discard the skins and stones left in the sieve. You will need 700ml/1¼ pints of purée.
- Pour the purée over the ingredients in the baking dish, mix well, then cover the dish with foil and leave at room temperature for 12 hours.
- Preheat the oven to 130°C/250°F/gas mark 1 and remove the foil from the baking dish. Bake the mincemeat for 2½ hours.
- Mix in the amaretto, then spoon into warm, sterilized jars, prodding regularly as you do so to remove any air bubbles.

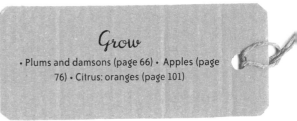

Grow
• Plums and damsons (page 66) • Apples (page 76) • Citrus: oranges (page 101)

Store in a cool, dry, dark place
Keeps for a year or more

Pear caramel

The delicate flavour of pears is intensified in this gorgeous caramel sauce, which is based loosely on a traditional Belgian preserve called sirop de Liège. Use it instead of maple or golden syrup, particularly for drizzling over pancakes. Pear caramel loses its flavour if kept in the refrigerator, and does not last long once open, so use lots of small jars or bottles rather than one big one.

MAKES 700–800ML/1¼–1½ PINTS

INGREDIENTS
- 1kg/2lb 3oz pears, peeled, cored and roughly sliced
- 450g/1lb apples (dessert or cooking), peeled, cored and roughly sliced
- 200g/7oz light muscovado sugar
- 100g/3½oz dark muscovado sugar

METHOD
- Place the apples and pears, including their peel and cores, into a large pan and add just a splash of water, enough to lift the fruit off the base and stop it sticking.
- Simmer very gently over a low heat for an hour or until the fruit is very soft and disintegrating.
- Mash the fruit gently, then put it into a jelly bag placed in a clean pan.
- Squeeze the jelly bag gently to extract a smooth liquid without allowing too much pulp into the pan, but there is no need to worry about the juice being clear. There should be 700–800ml/1¼–1½ pints of liquid. Discard the contents of the jelly bag.
- Add the sugar to the liquid and set the pan over a low heat. Bring to a slow simmer, stirring to dissolve the sugar, then continue to simmer for 30 minutes until thickened and syrupy. (It will thicken further as it cools.)
- Pour into warm, sterilized bottles, and seal.

Store in a cool, dry, dark place; give the jar a good shake before using each time
Keeps for six months; once opened, 2–4 weeks

Grow
- Pears (page 86)
- Apples (page 76)

Growing grapes

It is perhaps due to the antiquity of grapes as a crop that their cultivation is so shrouded in impenetrable jargon, but grapevines are actually much more accessible for the home grower than their mysteriousness would suggest. These plants tolerate most conditions, but for optimum harvests follow the few simple guidelines below.

BEST VARIETIES

Grapevines are divided into two types: dessert (eating) and wine ones. The former have been bred from the latter to provide larger, sweeter and firmer grapes more suitable for transporting across the world. When growing your own, choose wine varieties: you will get a much wider flavour palette in the grapes and, if you are growing outdoors, a more reliable harvest.

Black grape varieties worth growing include 'Boskoop Glory', 'Pinot Noir' and 'Concord Seedless'; for white grapes try 'Siegerrebe' and 'Phönix'.

PLANTING

Grapevines are usually sold as potted plants – put them in the ground in autumn or preferably spring when the coldest frosts have passed. Set them in the sunniest spot you have – trained against a sunny wall or fence is ideal. You could also grow grapevines in a greenhouse, either as a standard in a pot or trained on a framework. However, unless your greenhouse is large, I would plant the grapevine outside and leave the greenhouse to crops that actually need it.

There are all sorts of complicated systems for growing grapevines, but you will still get plenty of fruit and a healthy plant by training each as a cordon/espalier hybrid (see also page 15). Fix the supporting wires, spaced 30cm/12in apart, before you plant.

MAINTENANCE

For training on a wall/frame allow a single central stem to grow upwards – as tall as you like – and from this stem tie in side shoots to the adjacent supporting wires, removing any side shoots from the stem that fall between these wires. Every winter, cut the side shoots back to two buds away from the central stem.

It is a good idea to prune in summer as well, to improve air circulation, thereby reducing the likelihood of infection from diseases such as mildew. Such summer pruning also allows more light to the fruit, ripening it faster. Snip off the ends of the side shoots so that there is only one bunch of grapes per side shoot, and remove the leaves around the bunches as well (use them for dolmades).

Standard grapevines will need a large pot and a strong cane for support. Keep a clear stem of 1m/3ft and then allow five or six branches at the top to form a lollipop shape. Shorten these branches to two buds in the winter and five leaves in the summer. You may also need to tie the branches to the cane to help support the weight of the grapes.

Water the grapevine well in its first year, and in very dry spells, but otherwise it will need no water or extra fertilizers unless it is growing in a pot.

HARVEST

The grapes are ready when they are a little soft, sweet and fully coloured, and the seeds (if appropriate) are brown. The bunch will ripen from the top down, so test the ones at the bottom before picking in late summer to autumn; slightly unripe fruit can be used for preserving.

Use in:
• Grape jelly (page 93)
• Mostarda di frutta (page 88)

Grape jelly

This jelly is so versatile that it is just as comfortable completing a peanut butter and jelly sandwich as it is accompanying roast poultry. Green grapes make a stunning golden yellow jelly, while black grapes turn it deep crimson. Grape jelly is ideal for using those bunches that haven't fully ripened before they need harvesting.

MAKES ABOUT 1.3KG/2LB 14OZ

INGREDIENTS
- 1kg/2lb 3oz grapes, de-stalked
- 1 large cooking apple, peeled, cored and roughly sliced
- 1 lemon, juiced
- granulated sugar (75g per 100ml/2½oz per 3½fl oz of juice; see method)

METHOD
- Put the grapes, apple slices and lemon juice into a large pan. Add enough cold water to cover the fruit.
- Bring to a gentle simmer and cook, uncovered, until the grapes and apple slices are easily crushed with a potato masher.
- Mash the fruit well, then pour the entire contents of the pan into a jelly bag placed in a large bowl.
- Hang up the jelly bag to drip into the bowl, and leave for at least 3 hours, preferably overnight.
- Discard the contents of the jelly bag and measure the juice.
- Pour the juice into a clean pan with the appropriate amount of sugar. Heat gently, stirring until all the sugar dissolves. Then turn up the heat and boil rapidly until the setting point (see Testing for a set, page 32) is reached.
- Remove from the heat and discard any scum from the jelly, then pot into warm, sterilized jars.

Grow
- Grapes (page 92)
- Apples (page 76)
- Citrus: lemons (page 101)

Store in a cool, dry, dark place
Keeps for a year or more

Damson jelly

Damson jam, considered by many as the king of jams for its deeply-fruity flavour, was a staple addition to my childhood porridge. However it is virtually impossible to get all the stones out as damsons cook, and it is a real faff to pit the raw fruit, whereas damson jelly is guaranteed stone-free. Don't limit its use to sweet dishes though – it is equally good with rich meats such as game.

MAKES ABOUT 900G/2LB

INGREDIENTS
- 1kg/2lb 3oz damsons
- granulated sugar (75g per 100ml/2½oz per 3½fl oz of juice; see method)

METHOD
- Put the damsons in a large pan and add cold water until the fruit is just covered. Simmer without a lid over a medium to low heat until the fruit is very tender (up to an hour), then mash roughly with a potato masher.
- Pour the entire contents of the pan into a jelly bag set in a bowl. Hang up the jelly bag to drip into the bowl and leave it for at least 3 hours, preferably overnight.
- Discard the contents of the jelly bag and measure the juice.
- Pour the juice into a clean pan with the appropriate amount of sugar. Heat gently, stirring to dissolve the sugar, then turn up the heat and bring to the boil.
- Boil rapidly until a setting point is reached (see Testing for a set, page 32), then remove from the heat, scrape off any scum and pot into warm, sterilized jars.

Something a little different

SPICED DAMSON JELLY
While developing this recipe I wrote in my notes 'Can't stop eating it, like Christmas in a jar', which I think tells you everything you need to know.
- Add 2 cinnamon sticks, 1 star anise and ½ tsp ground allspice to the damsons as they simmer.

DAMSON AND ORANGE JELLY
Just a hint of orange comes through in the final jelly.
- Add the pared peel of 2 oranges (avoid including the white pith) to the damsons as they simmer.

Store in a cool, dry, dark place
Keeps for a year or more

Growing quinces

Quinces, not oranges, were the fruit in the original marmalade (*marmelo*) paste from Portugal. In their raw form, quinces are completely inedible – hard and gritty, with a downy fluff all over their yellow skins. However this does mean that the fruits will last for ages once picked ('bombproof' is how one grower described them to me). When cooked, they have a delicious, honeyed taste. Quinces are also wonderfully ornamental garden trees, with great, if irregular, shapes, and to my mind they produce the prettiest of spring fruit blossoms.

BEST VARIETIES

All quinces are self-fertile so you will need only one tree, which will provide more than enough fruit. It may be difficult to source specific varieties, but there is little difference between them anyway, so buy whichever named variety is available. Do not confuse these quinces (*Cydonia oblonga*) with Japanese quince (*Chaenomeles*), which is also edible, but not nearly as nice.

PLANTING

Plant bare-root trees in the dormant season or potted specimens in autumn or spring, in a sheltered, sunny spot. They are not easily trained or restricted, so set in open ground if possible, although a very large pot would suffice for a few years at least.

MAINTENANCE

Mulch annually. Once mature, prune only to remove the 4Ds (see page 16) in winter and ensure no fruit is left rotting on the branches.

HARVEST

Pick once the fruit has turned completely yellow and is already aromatic, in mid- or late autumn. It is worth gathering a few just to leave in a bowl – their fragrance easily perfumes a whole room, and is even strong enough to scent other fruit, so avoid storing them with apples and pears.

Use in:
- Membrillo (page 98)
- Pâté de fruit (page 100)

Membrillo

It slices like cheese, can be shaped like cheese, is often sold on a cheese counter, and indeed should be eaten with cheese, but it's not *actually* cheese. Membrillo, or quince cheese, is a solid jelly, made and stored in a mould, and then turned out to be sliced. The choice of moulds is entirely up to you – most things will do, though smaller vessels such as ramekins mean you have to unmould less at a time. I favour the mini-loaf tins usually used for cakes. The final colour of the membrillo will depend on the fruit (specifically their tannin levels) and how long it takes to reach the right consistency.

MAKES ABOUT 1KG/2LB 3OZ

INGREDIENTS
- 1kg/2lb 3oz quinces, de-fluffed and roughly chopped
- granulated sugar (125g/4oz per 150ml/¼ pint of purée; see method)
- unflavoured oil (e.g. sunflower or canola)

METHOD
- Put the prepared quinces into a large pan and add water so the fruit is only just submerged. Bring to a simmer, uncovered, over a medium heat.
- Continue to simmer gently, stirring occasionally, until the fruit is soft and breaking up into a pulp (about an hour).
- Rub the contents of the pan through a sieve, then measure the purée. Discard the skins and cores in the sieve.
- Put the purée in a clean pan, together with the appropriate amount of sugar.
- Heat gently, stirring to dissolve the sugar. Bring to a gentle simmer, then cook uncovered, stirring frequently to prevent the purée from sticking to the base of the pan. Simmer until the purée is much reduced and so thick that it can be parted on the pan base; this could take 1–2 hours.
- Meanwhile coat the inside of each mould with a thin layer of the oil, applied with a pastry brush or piece of kitchen paper; be sure to get right into any mould corners. Cut a piece of nonstick baking paper to fit the top of each mould exactly.
- Pour the purée into the moulds and smooth down the appropriate piece of baking paper over the top, so there are no air bubbles beneath. If the moulds have no lids, once they are cool wrap them tightly in clingfilm. Ideally, store for a month before using to allow the flavour to develop.

Store in a cool, dry, dark place; once unmoulded/opened, keep in the refrigerator
Keeps for a year

Grow
- Quinces (page 96)

Pâté de fruit

Pâté de fruit is a popular French confection and has its origins in comfits, which were the original fruit pastilles – being small pieces of jellied fruit rolled in sugar. Any fruit can be used to make pâté de fruit, but I think the delicate flavours of quince and pear work particularly well in this way. Serve a plateful as petits fours at the end of a meal.

Something a little different

BERRY FLAVOURS

Any single berry type or a mix of types can be used. Purée 500g/1lb 2oz fresh berries (sieve to remove the seeds if preferred) and put into a pan with 500g/1lb 2oz granulated sugar and 30g/1oz powdered pectin or 30ml/1fl oz liquid pectin. Bring to the boil and cook as above.

MAKES 40–50 SWEETS

INGREDIENTS
- 600g/1lb 5oz quinces, de-fluffed and chopped, or pears, roughly chopped
- unflavoured oil (e.g. sunflower or canola)
- granulated sugar (an equal weight to the pulp; see method)
- 30g/1oz powdered pectin or 30ml/1fl oz liquid pectin

METHOD
- Put the fruit in a large pan with cold water to a depth of about 2.5cm/1in. Cover and simmer over a low heat, stirring occasionally, until the fruit is very soft (the quinces will take much longer than pears).
- Meanwhile line a shallow baking tin, approximately 10 × 15cm/4 × 6in, with nonstick baking paper and brush with a thin layer of the oil. Alternatively use silicone confectionery moulds to make, for example, individual spheres, but these too need oiling.
- Rub the entire contents of the pan through a sieve, discarding the peel and cores left behind. Weigh the pulp and put in a clean pan with an equal weight of sugar, then add the pectin.
- Whisk immediately and continue whisking as you bring the mixture slowly to the boil over a medium heat.
- Once the sugar has dissolved and the pectin is properly mixed in, continue to boil the pulp until it reaches setting point (see Testing for a set, page 32), stirring constantly with a wooden spoon to stop it catching – be careful, the pulp can spit.
- Pour the pulp into the lined baking tin to a level layer 1–2cm/½–¾in thick, or into the moulds. Leave to set.
- Once solidified, cut the confectionery into small squares or diamonds using a hot, dry knife (dip it in boiling water and dry), or unmould, if appropriate. Toss each sweet in caster sugar and store in an airtight tin or box filled with more caster sugar.

Grow
- Quinces (page 96) • Pears (page 86)
- Strawberries (page 36) • Raspberries, blackberries and hybrid berries (page 52) • Blueberries (page 60)
- Gooseberries (page 40)

Store in a cool, dry place
Keeps for 3–4 months

Growing citrus fruits

The citrus family is large and varied, but its cultivation requirements are the same for all the main fruits: lemons, oranges, limes and grapefruits. In good conditions, these plants can produce flowers and fruits year-round (and at the same time), and it is worth having them somewhere you can really appreciate their fabulous fragrance.

BEST VARIETIES

For lemons, the compact and relatively hardy *Citrus × limon* 'Meyer' is one of the most widely available; try *C. × aurantiifolia* (Persian or Tahiti lime) for limes, as this variety is tolerant of cold weather. *Citrus × aurantium* Sweet Orange Group 'Baia' (syn. *C. sinensis* 'Washington') is a good orange, and *C. × aurantium* Grapefruit Group 'Marsh' a good grapefruit. All are self-fertile. Assuming you will be growing your citrus plant in a large pot, all of these should be on a dwarfing rootstock.

PLANTING

Given its need for frost protection, a large pot is generally the best planting option for a citrus tree in temperate climates, because you can move it between a sunny patio in summer and a light greenhouse or conservatory in winter. Avoid centrally heated rooms as these dry the plant out too much. Citrus plants will be supplied in a pot, rarely bare root. Use multipurpose or specific citrus compost and the largest pot you can safely move, and repot the tree every couple of years to replenish the compost.

MAINTENANCE

A citrus tree does not need much pruning: just remove the 4Ds (see page 16) in late spring (once there is little risk of frosts) and any branches necessary to keep it to a manageable size and to form a pleasing shape. Its rootstock may produce suckers, so remove these to the lowest point possible.

Water as required and do not allow the soil to dry out, as this may cause the tree to shed any fruit. During winter a citrus tree will still need watering, but considerably less than in summer.

Apply fertilizer in spring and summer, but do not add it to the water every time, in order to avoid a build-up of salts. There are some specific citrus fertilizers but otherwise buy a fertilizer that contains all the trace elements and has a high nitrogen (N) and medium potassium (K) ratio.

HARVEST

Fruit can ripen year-round. When ready for harvesting, the fruit will be well-coloured and aromatic. Cut it off the branch, keeping a short stem on the fruit; never pull off the fruit.

Use in:
- Lemon curd (page 102)
- Apple pie curd (page 80)
- Windfall marmalade (page 78)
- Greengage jam (page 68)
- High Dumpsideary jam (page 75)
- Black butter (page 84)

Lemon curd

Being zingy, zesty and a bright sunshine yellow, this recipe is all you want from a lemon curd. Spread it on toast, use it in desserts (it is particularly good with a summer berry pavlova) or eat it straight out of the jar – it's up to you.

MAKES ABOUT 500G/1LB 2OZ

INGREDIENTS
- 3 lemons, zest and juice
- 3 eggs
- 75g/2½oz unsalted butter, cubed
- 150g/5oz caster sugar

METHOD
- Add the lemon zest and juice to a ceramic or glass bowl with the other ingredients.
- Set the bowl over a pan of simmering water on a medium heat – the bowl should fit snugly over the pan but not touch the water itself.
- Use a whisk to incorporate all the ingredients (flecks of unmelted butter are fine at this stage).
- With a wooden spoon (metal implements can taint the taste), stir continuously for 10–15 minutes – stirring from side to side incorporates the ingredients faster and more effectively than going round and round. Once the butter has melted, simply keep the mixture moving off the base of the bowl, to prevent the eggs from scrambling.
- The curd is ready when it coats the back of the spoon, and a track remains when you draw your finger through the mixture. It will thicken further as it cools.
- Pot into warm, sterilized jars.

Grow
Citrus: lemons and limes
(page 101)

Store in the refrigerator
Keeps for a month or so

Something a little different

LEMON, HONEY AND GINGER CURD
This is the classic herbal tea in curd form, just the thing for a nasty cold.
- Substitute 150g/5oz of honey (use local, artisan honey if you can, as it will add more flavour) for the caster sugar, and add 3 tbsp peeled and freshly grated ginger root. For a bigger ginger hit, add more grated ginger to taste.

LIME CURD
This is even zingier than the lemon curd, and works really well with dark chocolate. It does not come out green though, so you could add some food colouring if you wanted.
- Use 6 limes in place of the 3 lemons.

Growing medlars

I always feel a bit sorry for medlars as they are not popular – probably due to their unattractive appearance, generally likened to a dog's bottom. However they do deserve more recognition not only as a delicious, low-maintenance fruit – especially for preserving – but also as a beautiful ornamental tree.

BEST VARIETIES
There is really little difference between the medlar varieties in terms of flavour, and the choice at many nurseries is usually limited to only one variety. If you can find either of them, 'Large Russian' and 'Dutch' have bigger fruits than other varieties. Check the rootstock is 'Quince A' or 'BA29', as these will produce the healthiest, best-sized trees (4–6m/13–20ft high and wide).

PLANTING
Plant bare-root trees in the dormant season, and potted ones in autumn or spring. It is not possible to train medlar trees, so you need plenty of open ground for their spreading habit. They will tolerate some shade and most soils if well-drained. At the time of planting, stake each medlar tree.

MAINTENANCE
Mulch and apply a controlled-release fertilizer in spring, and water in very dry spells, especially while the tree is establishing.

A little pruning in the first few years to create a good framework is all medlars need; thereafter remove the 4Ds as necessary (see page 16).

HARVEST
Pick medlars from mid- to late autumn, once the fruits are at least 2.5cm/1in across. They will need bletting: setting on a plate so they do not touch and each 'eye' is downwards, and leaving in a cool, dry place, until soft. Check regularly for signs of rot and dispose of infected fruit. Some gardeners recommend leaving the fruit on the tree until after a heavy frost, so that the weather blets the fruit for you, but this is a riskier strategy.

Use in:
• Medlar fudge (page 105)

Medlar fudge

This is my version of an ancient recipe that, although called fudge, bears no resemblance to the modern confection. Medlar fudge is a sweet, boozy, spiced paste and is traditionally served folded into whipped cream with shortbread biscuits crumbled over the top. You can also drizzle it with honey, but I would recommend that only if you have a very sweet tooth!

MAKES ABOUT 550G/1LB 4OZ

INGREDIENTS
- 1kg/2lb 4oz medlars, roughly chopped
- 2 lemons, roughly chopped
- 2 cloves
- 1 cinnamon stick
- 500ml/1 pint cider
- light muscovado sugar (70g/2½oz per 100g/3½oz of pulp; see method)

METHOD
- Put the chopped medlars and lemons into a large pan with the spices and cider. Bring to a gentle simmer and continue simmering, uncovered, until the medlars are soft (about 45 minutes).
- Mash the fruit with a potato masher.
- Push the entire contents of the pan through a sieve and weigh the pulp (discard what is left in the sieve).
- Return the pulp to a clean pan, together with the appropriate amount of sugar. Stir until you have a smooth, chocolate-brown paste.
- Bring to the boil over a medium heat and, once it reaches boiling point, pot immediately into warm, sterilized jars.

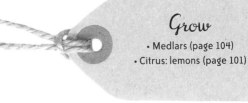

Grow
- Medlars (page 104)
- Citrus: lemons (page 101)

Store in a cool, dry, dark place
Keeps for six months or more

FROM
THE VEG
GARDEN

SPRING AND SUMMER

Growing rhubarb

If I had to pick one crop that was totally fail-safe, something that was virtually indestructible and on which you could rely to produce a good crop every year, it would be rhubarb. Although generally considered a fruit for its use in sweet dishes in the kitchen, it is technically a perennial vegetable, because it is the stems that are eaten. The leaves are poisonous but perfectly safe to compost.

BEST VARIETIES
The early varieties such as 'Timperley Early' and 'Champagne' are best for forcing (see right), and produce good tender stems. For really red stems, try 'Holstein Bloodred' or 'Cawood Delight'.

PLANTING
Plants are available potted and also as bare lumps of woody root (called 'crowns') in bags. The former plants are likely to be healthier, if more expensive. If you have a friend with a large plant, the crowns can also be chopped into large chunks with a sharp spade, and the pieces replanted. Plant bare crowns in autumn or early spring while the crown is still dormant; potted plants can be put in the ground from autumn until late spring.

Use in:
• Pickled rhubarb (page 110) • Rhubarb and rosemary ketchup (page 112)

Rhubarb will grow in almost full shade, but ideally likes a rich, moist soil in full sun. The crown should be just level with the soil – too low and it may rot.

MAINTENANCE
Apart from watering in very dry spells, rhubarb plants need little attention. Cut off any flower spikes at the base, to allow maximum energy storage in the crown for the following season. Remove all the dead leaves in autumn, to expose the crown to the cold weather it needs during winter in order to crop well the following spring. Give rhubarb a mulch of compost in spring, but do not cover the crown itself.

HARVEST
Stems on unforced plants will be ready from mid-spring, and can be taken until midsummer. Always pull the stems, do not cut them. If a stem does not detach easily from the crown, it is not ready for harvesting. Never take all the stems from a single plant – it needs some to photosynthesize and store energy for next year. It is also wise not to harvest from a plant in its first year.

FORCING RHUBARB
For tender, bright pink stems in early spring, you can force rhubarb plants. This can be done in late winter by covering each crown with an upturned dustbin or anything else that excludes all light – traditional terracotta forcing pots are attractive but expensive. The stems can be harvested once they reach the top of the bin/pot.

Do not force a plant in its first year, and do not do this to the same plant two years running. The process takes a lot of energy from the plant, and it needs time to establish after planting, and time to recover after forcing. Similarly do not take further stems from the plant after all the forced ones have been harvested.

Pickled rhubarb

Even if the idea of eating raw rhubarb sets your teeth on edge, I would still encourage you to try this pickle. This recipe uses the first, most tender rhubarb stems of the season – ideally forced if you have them, otherwise the slenderest, pinkest ones you can find. My favourite use for pickled rhubarb is with a dinner of raclette cheese melted over potatoes, using the eponymous table-top grill.

MAKES ABOUT 300G/10OZ

INGREDIENTS
- 300g/10oz rhubarb, preferably forced
- 1½ tsp black peppercorns
- 3 juniper berries
- 3 tsp coriander seeds
- 90ml/3fl oz cider vinegar
- 2 tbsp water
- 45g/1½oz caster sugar
- 1 tsp fine sea salt

METHOD
- Cut the rhubarb stems into uniform pieces 2cm/¾in long.
- Pack the stems on end into a sterilized jar and add the peppercorns, juniper berries and coriander seeds.
- Put the vinegar, water, sugar and salt into a small pan and bring to the boil, stirring to dissolve the sugar and salt.
- Once they are dissolved and the liquid is boiling, pour it into the jar so that the rhubarb is completely submerged (tap the base of the jar gently on the work surface to dislodge any air bubbles) but there is still a clear 1cm/½in gap between the liquid and the rim.
- Seal immediately, and leave to mature for 2 days before eating.

Grow
- Rhubarb (page 109)
- Coriander (page 154)

Store in the refrigerator
Keeps for a month or more

Rhubarb and rosemary ketchup

If you have run out of tomato and plum ketchups (pages 128 and 70) by early spring, this rhubarb version will restock your cupboards nicely. You can make it with forced or unforced stems, and it is a good recipe for using up less tender shoots, but the pinker the stems the pinker the ketchup. The rosemary pairs beautifully with the rhubarb to create a savoury, sweet-and-sour sauce.

MAKES ABOUT 700ML/1¼ PINTS

INGREDIENTS
- 8 sprigs of fresh rosemary, 15cm/6in long
- 4 garlic cloves
- ½ tbsp olive oil
- 1 red onion, finely diced
- 1kg/2lb 3oz rhubarb, trimmed and chopped into 2cm/¾in pieces
- 75ml/2½fl oz cider vinegar
- 1 tsp salt
- 100g/3½oz granulated sugar

METHOD
- Remove the leaves from the rosemary sprigs and finely chop, then pound them in a pestle and mortar with the garlic and oil until the garlic is crushed. Add the onion. (Alternatively, blitz the rosemary, garlic and oil together in a food processor with the onion.)
- Put the mixture into a large pan and braise very gently over a low heat until the onion is soft, stirring often.
- Add the rhubarb pieces to the mixture and stir well.
- Continue to cook over a low heat, stirring regularly to prevent sticking, until the rhubarb is completely broken down and a little reduced.
- Blend the entire contents of the pan into a smooth liquid, using a liquidizer or food processor, or rub it through a sieve.
- Put the liquidized mixture into a clean pan, together with the vinegar, salt and sugar.
- Bring to the boil, then reduce the heat and simmer, stirring occasionally, until the ketchup is thick but can still be poured (it will thicken further as it cools).
- Pour the ketchup into warm, sterilized bottles.

Grow
- Rhubarb (page 109)
- Rosemary (page 156)
- Garlic (page 121)
- Onions (page 129)

Store in a cool, dry, dark place; once opened, keep in the refrigerator
Keeps for six months or more

Growing carrots

Pulling up the first carrots of the year is like digging up buried treasure. The golden-coloured roots reveal themselves as the crushed foliage in my hand gives off that unmistakable carrot scent. Then I rush to the kitchen, anxious to cook them before too many of those precious sugars convert to starch.

BEST VARIETIES

Early and baby varieties provide the most tender roots for making smooth jams, and they can be sown at least twice during the growing season – the first harvest being replaced by another sowing. 'Chantenay' and 'Paris Market Baron' are good examples of this type. However longer-rooted varieties are easier to prepare, and are often sweeter. Try the 'Nantes' types, especially 'Early Nantes 2', which is an early carrot with a cylindrical root and exceptional flavour.

PLANTING

Sow direct into drills from early spring onwards, making the last sowing in midsummer. To avoid stumpy and forked carrots, sow in as light and well-drained a soil as possible, with minimal stones and organic matter: sow in deep pots if necessary.

MAINTENANCE

Thin the seedlings to a spacing of 5cm/2in. Water regularly, but do not overwater as this encourages foliage growth at the expense of roots. The only guaranteed protection from carrot fly is a constant, complete covering of horticultural fleece, but planting near onion crops and minimizing the handling of the foliage all help to mask the carroty smell that attracts the flies.

HARVEST

Carrots should be ready to start digging up two months after sowing. Pull a test root to see if it is big enough.

Use in:

- Carrot jam (page 114)
- Giardiniera (page 138)
- Pesto (page 158)
- Pickled cucumber (page 134)

Carrot jam

Carrots make a delicious sweet jam, especially from fresh roots that still have most of their natural sugars. (The longer the time since harvesting carrots, the greater the proportion of the sugars that will have been converted to starch.) When lightly spiced with cinnamon, ginger and orange – the classic carrot cake flavourings – carrot jam is delicious on a brioche bun, with cream cheese.

MAKES ABOUT 750G/1LB 10OZ

INGREDIENTS
- 450g/1lb peeled and trimmed carrots, grated
- 2 oranges, zest and juice
- 450ml/16fl oz water
- 400g/14oz granulated sugar
- 1 tsp ground cinnamon
- ½ tsp ground ginger

METHOD
- Put the grated carrots into a large pan, together with the orange zest and juice and the water. Cover and bring to the boil, then simmer gently until the carrots are soft.
- Blend the entire contents of the pan to a smooth purée, using a liquidizer or food processor.
- Put the purée into a clean pan and add the sugar and spices. Bring to the boil slowly, over a medium heat, stirring to dissolve the sugar.
- Turn down the heat and simmer gently, stirring frequently to stop the mixture catching on the base of the pan. It is ready when it parts easily on the base of the pan and feels thicker – this will take about 15 minutes.
- Pot the jam into warm, sterilized jars.

Grow
- Carrots (page 113)
- Citrus: oranges (page 101)

Store in a cool, dry, dark place
Keeps for a year or more

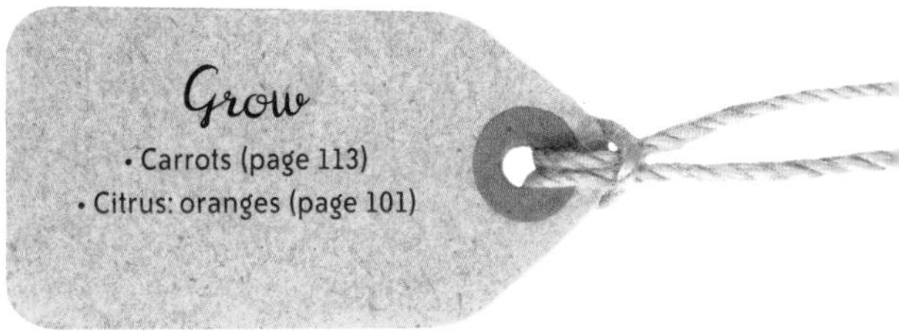

Growing beetroot

Until I started growing my own food, I didn't care for beetroot. But then I made the novice's error of growing something I did not eat just because I had some free seeds – and I haven't looked back. Besides, what's not to like? Beetroot is super easy to grow, reliable and low-maintenance, comes in a huge range of colours and flavours, and provides you not only with roots but also with leafy green tops for salads.

BEST VARIETIES

For beginners I would always recommend 'Boltardy' for its reliability, but other good red-rooted varieties include 'Cylindra' (with long roots rather than rounded ones, as the name suggests), 'Sanguina' and 'Detroit Dark Red'. The candy-striped 'Chioggia' has a more pronounced earthy flavour, while 'Burpee's Golden' is my favourite for yellow roots.

PLANTING

Sow thinly in drills from early spring onwards, even though earlier sowings are more likely to bolt (run to seed) in hot, dry conditions. Beetroot does not need as light a soil as carrots (page 113) and prefers full sun, but does tolerate partial shade. It also grows happily in containers.

MAINTENANCE

Wait until the seedlings have reached a small, but usable size and then thin to a spacing of 10cm/4in; otherwise you can thin the roots earlier and use only the tops for salads. Water well, especially in hot weather, to deter plants from bolting. Mulching the tops of the roots as they appear above the soil surface is beneficial but not essential.

HARVEST

As soon as the roots are big enough, start gathering your crop. Do this by taking out every other root, rather than a section of a row, and leaving the rest of the beets to mature into the vacated spaces. Use a hand fork or trowel to lever each one out gently, to avoid breaking the root.

Use in:
- Beetroot chutney (page 118)
- Red chrain (page 120)

Beetroot chutney

This fruity, earthy and lightly spiced chutney has a fabulous deep red colour – providing you use red beetroot of course. It is particularly good with cold meats and fish, and a new potato salad. If you can grind your own coriander from home-grown or bought seeds, so much the better.

MAKES ABOUT 1.5KG/3LB 5OZ

INGREDIENTS
- 1kg/2lb 3oz beetroot, peeled
- 300g/10oz red onions, peeled
- 650g/1lb 7oz cooking apples, peeled and cored
- 500ml/17½fl oz red wine vinegar
- 450g/1lb granulated sugar
- 1 tsp mixed spice
- ½ tsp ground coriander
- 2 oranges, zest and juice

METHOD
- Dice the beetroot, onions and apples, trying to keep all the dice roughly the same size across the different ingredients.
- Put the diced ingredients into a large pan, together with the vinegar, sugar and spices, and stir well to mix them all together.
- Cook over a low–medium heat at a very gentle simmer, stirring regularly for about 2 hours, or until you can part the mixture on the base of the pan.
- Add the orange zest and juice and mix them in well.
- Cook for a further 5–10 minutes until once again the mixture can be parted on the base of the pan and there is very little free liquid.
- Pot the chutney into warm, sterilized jars and leave to mature for a month before using.

Grow
- Beetroot (page 116)
- Apples (page 76)
- Red onions (page 129)
- Citrus: oranges (page 101)

Store in a cool, dry, dark place
Keeps for a year or more

Red chrain

This relish/pickle is traditionally served at Passover with fish, but its earthy sweetness and healthy kick from the horseradish also sit well with a burger. I like the crunch from the raw roots, but if you prefer a smoother texture you could blitz them in a food processor rather than grating them.

MAKES ABOUT 225G/8OZ

INGREDIENTS
- 200g/7oz beetroot, peeled and coarsely grated
- 75g/2½oz horseradish, peeled and coarsely grated
- 100ml/3½fl oz cider vinegar
- 2 tsp fine sea salt
- 2 tsp granulated sugar

METHOD
- Mix the grated beetroot and horseradish together well, then pack them into a warm, sterilized jar.
- Put the vinegar, salt and sugar into a small pan and bring to the boil, then pour immediately over the beetroot and horseradish already in the jar.
- Tap the jar on the work surface and prod the contents with a spoon to dislodge and release any air bubbles, then seal.

Grow
- Beetroot (page 116)
- Horseradish (page 155)

Store in the refrigerator
Keeps for a month or more

Growing garlic

Since it is probably one of the most essential vegetables in my kitchen, I wouldn't be without garlic. Growing your own allows you to enjoy it fresh (green garlic), use the stalks (scapes), grow bigger bulbs and create those long plaits of bulbs to hang in the window for an instant French farmhouse feel.

BEST VARIETIES

There are two types of garlic: hardneck and softneck. Softneck is the best choice for producing bulbs to dry and store, while either type can be pickled. 'Solent Wight' (softneck) and 'Lautrec Wight' (hardneck) are reliable and have good flavour. For bigger, milder cloves try elephant garlic (not technically a garlic, but similar in appearance and uses), which is rare in the shops, and may require a bigger pickling jar!

PLANTING

Garlic needs a period of cold weather to divide into the individual cloves and the longer it is in the ground the bigger the bulb will be, so plant in autumn or early winter. Spring plantings will more likely yield a single large clove, which is still delicious, but harder to fit into a jar when pickling (see page 122).

Grow garlic in light, well-drained soil in full sun. It can also be planted in pots; because it does not need a lot of depth, bulb pans are ideal. Break the bulb up into the individual cloves, and push them into the soil at 20cm/8in intervals (25cm/10in apart for elephant garlic), 2.5cm/1in deep in clay soils and 10cm/4in deep in sandy soils. The roots will develop from the flat end of the clove (the basal plate), so plant with this downwards.

MAINTENANCE

Keep the ground weed-free. Cut off any flower stalks as they appear (and eat them).

HARVEST

As the leaves begin to yellow, from early to midsummer, pull up the bulbs and leave them to dry in the sun for 2–3 days before preserving or hanging them for further drying. For a milder flavour, harvest as green garlic in late spring, but expect some sacrifice on the size of the cloves.

Use in:
- Pickled garlic (page 122)
- Plum ketchup (page 70)
- Rhubarb and rosemary ketchup (page 112) • Chilli jam (page 142)
- Sweet chilli dipping sauce (page 144) • Tomato ketchup (page 128)
- Pesto (page 158)

Pickled garlic

With its sweet-and-sour, crunchy, full-on garlic flavour, this recipe is one for garlic-lovers. Boiling the cloves briefly tempers the taste slightly, but nonetheless a little can go a long way! I slice the pickled cloves into pasta or risotto dishes, over pizza or add whole cloves to a roasting joint as it goes into the oven. The number of bulbs you need will depend on their size, so check how many cloves will fit into the jar before starting to cook, in case you require a few more.

MAKES ABOUT 225G/8OZ

INGREDIENTS
- 4–5 garlic bulbs
- 2 bay leaves
- 4 sprigs of rosemary, thyme and/or oregano, 15cm/6in long
- 150ml/¼ pint white wine vinegar
- 40g/1½oz granulated sugar

METHOD
- Peel and top and tail the garlic cloves, and put them in a small pan with all the other ingredients.
- Bring to the boil slowly over a medium heat, stirring to dissolve the sugar.
- Once the mixture is bubbling well, cook for 3 minutes, then remove from the heat.
- Remove the garlic cloves and herbs, using a slotted spoon, and layer them in a warm, sterilized jar.
- Pour in enough cooking liquid to cover the cloves completely, then seal the jar.

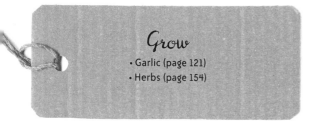

Grow
- Garlic (page 121)
- Herbs (page 154)

Store in the refrigerator
Keeps for a year or more

LATE SUMMER AND AUTUMN

Growing tomatoes

There really is no excuse for not growing your own tomatoes these days. Young plants are available in every garden centre and often supermarkets too, as well as seeds in a huge choice of varieties. You do not even need a garden because there are cultivars specifically for growing in hanging baskets and on windowsills. And like the apple in the Garden of Eden, once you have taken that first bite of a home-grown tomato, there really is no going back.

BEST VARIETIES

Variety choice will come down to your own personal favourites, but there are a few groups to consider. First check the growth habit: indeterminate/vine plants are those grown as a cordon – a tall plant with a single stem tied into a support; determinate/bush plants are bushier and can be grown more easily in a pot or basket. There are some varieties that will fare better outdoors, others that need a greenhouse or similar protection and some that will do fine outdoors but would prefer a greenhouse.

Use in:
- Tomato jam (page 127)
- Tomato ketchup (page 128)
- Green tomato jam (page 126)

Then decide what type(s) of tomato you want to grow: big beefsteaks, plum, salad or cherry? For preserving, the best groups are plum or cherry, and for a tomato jam that veers more towards the sweet than the savoury try 'Rosella' or 'Orange Paruche' – or 'Green Envy' for a Green tomato jam (see page 126).

PLANTING

Sow seeds under cover in late winter, and pot on before planting out after the last frost in early summer. Seeds need temperatures of at least 15°C/59°F to germinate. Alternatively buy young plants. All plants need hardening off (see page 20) before planting into pots, growbags or the open ground. Put in stakes to support cordon varieties.

MAINTENANCE

Tie in the stems of cordon varieties every 20–30cm/8–12in, and remove side shoots as they appear in the axils of fruit trusses and leaves off the main stem. Pinch out the main stem once it reaches the top of the stake. Keep well watered, and once the fruit starts to develop apply fertilizer regularly according to the manufacturer's instructions. Removing the lower leaves to allow more light to the fruit can also help ripening.

Blight is by far the biggest problem with tomatoes, especially on outdoor plants in humid, overcast summers. Keep an eye on the leaves and stems for brown, dead patches and discard the affected parts as soon as possible, burning them or removing from the garden. This may be enough to halt the spread, but, if not, take off any unaffected tomatoes (green ones can still be jammed – see Green tomato jam, page 126) and destroy the plant.

HARVEST

Pick as the fruit ripens to its final colour. Harvesting after midday will give the fruit the maximum concentrated flavour. If you are not able to use them straight away (always recommended), store them at room temperature – never in the refrigerator.

Green tomato jam

Of course we all want our tomatoes to ripen to beautiful shades of red, but sometimes nature has other ideas. If you have had to harvest your fruit while it is still green because of blight or early frosts, use it to make this zingy, herbaceous jam instead of the more usual chutney. Alternatively, grow a variety that is still green when ripe, such as 'Green Envy'.

MAKES ABOUT 1.4KG/3LB 1OZ

INGREDIENTS
- 1.2kg/2lb 10oz green tomatoes, halved
- 5 lemons
- 1kg/2lb 3oz granulated sugar

METHOD
- Scoop out each tomato's seedy innards, with a teaspoon, and put them into a jelly bag. Then finely chop the tomato flesh (use a food processor if you have one) and put it in a large pan.
- Finely grate the zest of the lemons and then juice them. Add the lemon zest to the pan, and put the squeezed-out lemon halves into the jelly bag.
- Pour the lemon juice into a measuring jug and top it up with water to give a total volume of 1.2 litres/ 2¼ pints. Add this liquid to the pan.
- Tie up the jelly bag and place it in the pan as well.
- Bring the pan mixture to a simmer and cook gently until the ingredients are soft (about 45 minutes).
- Wearing rubber gloves to protect your hands, remove the jelly bag and squeeze as much liquid as possible back into the pan. Discard the contents of the bag.
- Add the sugar and stir until it dissolves, then turn up the heat and bring the jam to the boil. Boil rapidly until the setting point is reached (see Testing for a set, page 32).
- Remove the pan from the heat and scrape off any scum. Then pot into warm, sterilized jars.

Store in a cool, dry, dark place
Keeps for a year or more

Tomato jam

I rather like this jam in a cheese sandwich, in place of fresh tomatoes when they are not in season. Like many preserves, this jam walks the line between sweet and savoury and how you use it will depend a lot on the variety of tomato you put in. The light muscovado sugar gives the flavour a caramel depth, but use granulated if you prefer.

MAKES ABOUT 1.2KG/2LB 10OZ

INGREDIENTS
- 1kg/2lb 3oz tomatoes, halved and deseeded
- 3 lemons, juiced
- 1 tsp fine sea salt
- 1 litre/1¾ pints water
- 1kg/2lb 3oz light muscovado sugar

METHOD
- Roughly chop the tomato flesh (no pieces too big as that will leave big bits of skin in the jam) and put into a large pan with the lemon juice, salt and water. Simmer over a low–medium heat until the tomatoes are soft, then mash thoroughly.
- Add the sugar and stir until it is dissolved, then turn up the heat and bring to the boil.
- Boil rapidly until the setting point is reached (see Testing for a set, page 32).
- Remove any scum and pot into warm, sterilized jars.

Grow
- Tomatoes (page 124)
- Citrus: lemons (page 101)

Store in a cool, dry, dark place
Keeps for a year or more

Tomato ketchup

Whether you eat it only on chips or, like Pop Larkin, smother everything on the plate at every meal, tomato ketchup is a staple food for many. Choose your paprika depending on what flavour you would like it to impart: smoked paprika gives it a (you guessed it) smoky edge; sweet paprika is the baseline paprika flavour; and hot smoked paprika has a bit of a kick.

MAKES ABOUT 400G/14OZ

INGREDIENTS

- 1kg/2lb 3oz tomatoes (off the vine weight)
- 4 garlic cloves, unpeeled
- 200ml/7fl oz cider vinegar
- 100g/3½oz light muscovado sugar
- 1 tsp fine sea salt
- black pepper, to taste
- ½ tsp paprika
- ¼ tsp ground cloves
- ¼ tsp ground allspice

METHOD

- Preheat the oven to 180°C/350°F/gas mark 4.
- Put the tomatoes and garlic cloves in a roasting tin (so that they fit snugly) and roast for 30 minutes.
- Pop the cloves out of their skins and blend with the tomatoes and their juices.
- Push the puréed tomatoes through a sieve into a medium-sized saucepan, to remove the seeds, then add the remaining ingredients.
- Stirring to dissolve the sugar, bring to a gentle simmer over a low heat. Continue simmering until the ketchup is reduced to a thick sauce. It should still be pourable – it will thicken further as it cools.
- Pour into warm, sterilized jars or bottles.

Grow
- Tomatoes (page 124)
- Garlic (page 121)
- Peppers (page 140)

Store in a cool, dry, dark place; once opened, keep in the refrigerator
Keeps for six months or more; once opened, lasts for two months

Something a little different

PEPPER
Substitute sweet peppers or the mild, smoky poblano chilli pepper for the tomatoes.
- Halve and remove the seeds, pith and stalk before roasting the sweet peppers.

Growing onions and shallots

Admittedly onions come pretty low on the list of 'must grow' vegetables, unless you are aiming for self-sufficiency. Generally it is hard to grow a basic white onion that tastes significantly better than a shop-bought one, and after buying sets or seed, and adding in your time, home-grown onions will come out much more expensive too. If you have only limited space, concentrate on other crops, but, if you can, grow red onions and shallots as they are much more worth the effort.

BEST VARIETIES

'Red Baron' is a widely available, reliable and tasty red onion, or else 'Electric'. For shallots, the chef's choice is 'Eschalote Grise' (not technically a shallot but sold as one) and 'Jermor' and 'Pikant' are also good choices. If you want to grow white onions, try 'Centurion'.

Use in:

• Caramelized onion marmalade (page 130) • Apple chutney (page 82) • Rhubarb and rosemary ketchup (page 112) • Beetroot chutney (page 118) • Tomato ketchup (page 128) • Giardiniera (page 138) • Sweetcorn relish (page 146) • Pumpkin chutney (page 150)

PLANTING

Onions and shallots need full sun, well-drained soil and good air circulation because humidity fosters fungal diseases, which can ruin the crop. For most varieties you have the choice of growing from seed or planting sets (small onions or shallots that have been grown and then stopped, ready for replanting and growing to maturity). Sets are by far the easiest choice, especially for cool-temperate areas, although they have a higher propensity to bolt if not heat-treated. On the other hand, you may not be able to get your desired cultivars as sets, and in fact long, thin shallots such as 'Eschalote Grise' are best grown from seed.

Sow seed in late winter under cover, then plant out in mid-spring, or just sow direct in mid-spring – sowing into modules or station sowing is best, thinning to the strongest seedling. Plant sets in autumn or early spring, pushing them into the ground to leave only the tip showing. For onions, leave 10cm/4in between plants and 30cm/12in between rows. Shallots should be spaced at 4cm/1½in between seeds, 15cm/6in between sets (sets will produce a larger cluster of bulbs, seeds a single bulb), and 20cm/8in between rows.

MAINTENANCE

Keep the rows weed-free. Water as required in dry weather, but avoid splashing the foliage and bulbs themselves, because this can encourage disease.

HARVEST

The foliage will start to yellow and die from mid- to late summer. Once this happens, pull up the onions/shallots (wait for a dry spell) and lay them out to dry in the sun, either on the soil, a bench or a piece of chicken wire suspended off the ground. The aim is to encourage good air circulation around each bulb as its outer layers dry in the sun; this should prevent rot setting in. Once dried for a few days they are ready to store in a cool, dry place.

Caramelized onion marmalade

This isn't really a marmalade in the true sense of the word, but the sweet, sticky reduction of onions that has come to be widely known by that name. It is also one of the few chutney-type preserves that is ready to eat straight away – and indeed is better the sooner you eat it. Use caramelized onion marmalade in a sandwich with meats or cheese, to glaze sausages cooked in the oven or as a filling for a savoury tart or quiche.

Note: Red onions are naturally sweeter than white onions, so require less additional sugar.

MAKES ABOUT 250G/8OZ

INGREDIENTS
- 2 tbsp olive oil
- 450g/1lb onions, finely sliced
- 1 garlic clove, crushed
- pinch of fine sea salt
- 6 sprigs of thyme, leaves only
- ¼ star anise
- 2 tbsp red wine vinegar
- 3 tbsp balsamic vinegar
- 2 tbsp dark muscovado sugar (1 tbsp if red onions are used)

METHOD
- Heat the oil in a heavy-based frying or saucepan over a low heat. Add the onions, garlic, salt, thyme and star anise and sweat very gently (do not let the onions brown) until very soft (this can take up to an hour). Stir regularly.
- Remove the star anise, and add the vinegars and sugar and continue to cook until the onions are caramelized and most of the liquid is gone.
- Pot into warm, sterilized jars.

Grow
- Onions (page 129)
- Garlic (page 121)
- Thyme (page 157)

Store in the refrigerator
Keeps for a month or more, but better eaten sooner

Growing French beans

Also known as green beans, these prolific plants will give plenty of pickings for pickles and for eating fresh. Purple- and white-podded varieties add colour to the garden, as well as to the plate and the pickle jar, and their pretty flowers are loved by bees.

BEST VARIETIES

Choose first how you want French beans to grow – dwarf varieties do well in pots and in rows, giving a heavy crop but not over such a long period as climbing varieties. However, by making two or three sowings from early spring of dwarf plants, and protecting them with horticultural fleece or cloches, you can have a good supply all summer and into autumn. Climbing French beans take up very little ground, especially if you grow them up a trellis, or even up your sweetcorn plants (see page 145). Having settled on the growth habit, you can then choose whether it should have a round or flat pod, and what colour the pods should be.

Good dwarf choices are: the green, flat-podded 'The Prince'; the green, round-podded 'Delinel'; the purple, round-podded 'Purple Teepee'; and the yellow/white, flat-podded 'Rocquencourt'. Climbers 'Cobra' and 'Blue Lake' are well-established, green, round-podded varieties, or you could try 'Kingston Gold' for its yellow/white, flat pods and 'Cosse Violette' for its purple, rounded ones.

PLANTING

French beans are frost tender. Sow in modules or pots under cover in mid-spring, potting on as necessary, and plant out once there is little risk of frost. Alternatively sow direct in late spring, station sowing in rows for dwarf beans and at the base of canes/hazel stakes or similar supports for climbers. Space dwarf beans 25cm/10in apart, and give them a small cane for support, tying them in as required. Two climbers per cane/stake is sufficient for a five- or six-stake wigwam. Plant two seeds per station and thin to the strongest plant.

MAINTENANCE

Other than watering, especially when flowering and fruiting, French beans need relatively little assistance. You may however need to help each climber get that initial twist around its cane, and to feed plants growing in pots. Also keep an eye out for slugs. If you are making early and late sowings, protect plants from frosts with cloches or tunnels of horticultural fleece or plastic.

HARVEST

The beans are best gathered often and when small, before the seeds inside begin to swell. Check over the plant regularly for any you may have missed, because if a pod of seeds begins to dry out it will signal to the plant to stop producing more pods. Cut the clusters of beans off any dwarf variety, to avoid pulling up the whole plant, and pick climbing French beans carefully.

Use in:

- Giardiniera (page 138)
- Pickle sticks (page 135)

Growing cucumbers

Cucumbers are prolific but tender crops and will not survive a frost, but it is just as possible to get a successful harvest when growing them outside as it is in a greenhouse. The smaller fruits and miniature versions used for pickled gherkins or cornichons may be harder to get hold of in shops, too, so it is worth growing a plant or two.

BEST VARIETIES
Varieties are split into types of fruit and those good for growing outside or under cover. Good outdoor cucumbers include 'Burpless Tasty Green' and 'Crystal Lemon'; for greenhouses try 'Petita'. Gherkin varieties to try are 'Venlo Pickling' and 'Vert Petit de Paris'.

PLANTING
Sow seed in modules under cover in mid-spring, giving the seeds temperatures of 18–20°C/64–8°F. Pot on into small pots once the roots start to appear at the bases of the modules. Harden off (see page 20) and plant out in early summer after the last frosts. Alternatively sow direct in pots or growbags in a greenhouse in late spring.

Cucumbers need a sunny, warm position and rich, moist (but not wet) soil. Incorporate plenty of compost into the soil if planting in the open ground, and mulch after planting with more compost. Cucumbers are best grown up a wigwam, stakes, wires or a trellis to save space, but they will need tying in gently every 30cm/12in or so, to the support.

MAINTENANCE
Keep the soil moist at all times and give the plants some liquid feed if growth or fruiting slows. Pinch out the tip of the stem when it reaches the top of the support, and reduce side shoots to seven leaves. If white blotches appear on the leaves (powdery mildew) remove the affected parts promptly, to avoid it spreading further. Cucumber mosaic virus, which causes the leaves to develop a yellow mosaic pattern and growth to become distorted, is not treatable, so remove the whole plant.

HARVEST
Cut cucumbers and gherkins once they have reached 10–15cm/4–6in long. If any shorter, they may be bitter; if larger than this, the skins thicken and the flavour lessens.

Use in:
- Pickled cucumber (page 134)
- Giardiniera (page 138)

Pickled cucumber

Cucumbers grow so fast and freely in the summer months that they are the ideal candidate for preserving. Whether you prefer thin slices or whole gherkins, pickled cucumbers are deservedly popular, and especially good with fish and fatty meats such as salmon pâté or fried chicken. Dill is a classic pairing flavour-wise, and also has health benefits because it helps us digest the naturally indigestible cucumber.

Grow
• Cucumbers (page 133)
• Carrots (page 113)
• French beans (page 132)
• Dill (page 155)

Store in the refrigerator
Keeps for six months, once opened lasts for a month

MAKES ABOUT 500G/1LB 2OZ
Note: The final quantity made will depend on how the cucumbers are sliced, if at all, and therefore the amount of space around them for liquid in the jar. If you have left-over liquid, store it in a jar in the refrigerator. Pour it over fresh sliced veg and leave for 2–3 hours to make a quick pickle.

INGREDIENTS
- 500g/1lb 2oz cucumbers
- 1½ tbsp fine sea salt
- 250ml/9fl oz cider vinegar
- ½ tbsp granulated sugar
- ½ tbsp black peppercorns
- 3 juniper berries (or more – 3 per jar)
- medium-sized bunch of fresh dill fronds

METHOD
- Prepare the cucumbers – nick off any knobbly bits, then slice larger cucumbers into rounds or sticks as you prefer. Smaller gherkins/cornichons can be left whole. Put the cucumbers into a ceramic or glass bowl and toss in the salt. Cover and leave at room temperature for 24 hours.
- Heat the vinegar, sugar, peppercorns and juniper berries in a small saucepan, stirring to dissolve the sugar. Bring to the boil, then remove the pan from the heat and leave the liquid to cool.
- Drain, rinse and pat dry the cucumber. Then pack the cucumber into a sterilized jar (or jars) with the dill, and pour over the cold liquid and seal. There should be a clear 1cm/½in of vinegar at the top of the jar, then a further 1cm/½in of space below the lid. Leave for a few days for the flavours to mellow.

Something a little different

PICKLE STICKS
Batons of cucumber and carrot (another natural pairing) can be pickled together with whole French beans and then served as snacks or as part of a spread.
- Use 165g/5½oz cucumbers, 165g/5½oz carrots and 165g/5½oz French beans.
- Peel and top and tail the carrots and top and tail the beans. Cut the cucumber and carrots into batons and trim the beans so that everything is to the height of your jar(s); they will then pack in neatly on end.

Growing cauliflower

Brassicas – the family that includes cauliflower, as well as broccoli and cabbages – and I have a difficult relationship. As a rule I prefer to keep my vegetable garden looking as natural as possible, but brassicas are a crop that absolutely must be protected from birds and butterflies, and I resent the plants for needing that mesh covering. But . . . the variety of crops they provide, especially the cauliflowers, make up for it. Just.

BEST VARIETIES

There are varieties of cauliflower that can mature in almost any month of the year, but I focus here on the autumn-harvesting types. 'Graffiti' is a purple variety, while 'White Rock' a reliable, white one. The miniature varieties such as 'Igloo' or 'Fremont' are a good choice for smaller spaces. 'Romanesco' is sometimes described as a broccoli, but to my mind it is a cauliflower. Its distinctive, pointed, lime-green florets are perfect for pickling.

PLANTING

Cauliflowers prefer a rich soil in full sun, so dig in plenty of compost before sowing or planting. Sow seeds in modules in mid-spring; plant out the seedlings once they have reached a good size. Alternatively station sow, thinning to the strongest seedling, with plants spaced 45cm/18in apart – 60cm/24in for larger cultivars (check the instructions on the seed packet). For miniature plants, allow 15cm/6in each way. Make sure plants are firmed in well and cover them as soon as they are planted out, or when the seedlings appear. Horticultural fleece or fine mesh will keep out cabbage white butterflies and pigeons – stretch it over hoops stuck in the ground and peg down securely – or else buy pre-made tunnels.

MAINTENANCE

Ensure that plants are well-watered, especially in hot, dry conditions to avoid bolting, and keep the weeds in check to avoid stunting the plants.

HARVEST

Once the curd (head) of a cauliflower has reached a good size, cut the stalk below it. Leaving the plant in the ground may encourage it to produce some smaller side shoots, or else you can dispose of the whole plant.

Use in:
- Giardiniera (page 138)

Giardiniera

Every culinary culture has its own version of a mixed vegetable pickle – the British have piccalilli, the Americans chow-chow. This Italian recipe for a clear pickle is very similar to the French version, and both are translated roughly as 'of the garden'. Any combination of vegetables can be used: the beauty is in the mixture and the colourful, fresh look each ingredient gives to the finished pickle.

Grow
- Carrots (page 113)
- Cauliflower (page 136)
- Cucumber (page 133)
- Onions and shallots (page 129)
- Sweet peppers (page 140)
- French beans (page 132)
- Herbs (page 154)

MAKES ABOUT 1.9KG/4LB 3OZ

INGREDIENTS
- 1kg/2lb 3oz mixed vegetables (a combination of some or all of carrots, cauliflower, baby onions or shallots, cucumber, sweet peppers and French beans)
- 3 tbsp fine sea salt
- 1 litre/1¾ pints cider vinegar
- 3 tbsp granulated sugar
- 1 tbsp black peppercorns
- 1 tsp coriander or fennel seeds or sprigs of fresh rosemary (1–2 per jar)

METHOD
- Prepare the vegetables into roughly bite-sized pieces: slice the carrots and cucumber lengthways into batons; break the cauliflower into small florets; cut the onions/shallots into quarters; remove the pith and seeds from the peppers and slice into lengths; and top and tail the beans.
- Put all the vegetables into a large ceramic or glass bowl and toss through the salt. Cover and leave at room temperature overnight (or for up to 24 hours).
- Drain the vegetables, rinse them thoroughly, then pat dry. Leaving them to dry further, put the remaining ingredients into a large pan and heat the vinegar mix gently, stirring to dissolve the sugar.
- Bring the vinegar mix to the boil, then add the vegetables.
- As soon as the ingredients return to the boil, scoop out the vegetables and pack (as tightly as possible) into warm, sterilized jars.
- Pour over the hot liquid and seal.
- Leave the jars to cool to room temperature before storing. Ideally leave the giardiniera for a day or two before eating, although it can be used straight away.

Note: If you have some liquid left over, store it in a jar in the refrigerator to make quick pickles (pour it over prepared vegetables and leave for an hour or two before serving) at a later date.

Store in the refrigerator
Keeps for three months or more

Growing chillies and sweet peppers

There is more to chillies than simple heat levels – they have real depth of flavour too. From the mild poblano types – try them in the pepper variation of Tomato ketchup (see page 128) – to the fruity habanero (Scotch bonnet) types, there is a chilli to suit all tastes and heat tolerances. Many growers have open days and festivals where you can buy the fruit – and also plants and seeds – and this can be a good way to discover your favourites. Likewise sweet peppers reveal a lot more variety from the seed catalogue than from the supermarket shelf.

BEST VARIETIES

I lean towards the medium–hot habaneros such as 'Apricot' and 'Trinity' for preserving. 'Cayenne Long Slim' is a good hot chilli, while 'Hungarian Hot Wax' or 'Hungarian Black' are other milder but flavoursome choices. Smoky poblano peppers are generally sold simply as 'Poblano' seeds.

If you are going to grow sweet peppers, choose the long, tapering types rather than the ubiquitous bell shapes. Good ones include 'Friggitello', 'Mohawk' (which matures early, making it ideal for temperate climates) and the baby pepper 'Minibel Orange'.

PLANTING

Sow peppers in late winter, indoors and preferably in a heated propagator as they need temperatures of at least 18°C/64°F to germinate. Alternatively buy young plants: specialist growers will have the widest variety range.

Plant out after the last frost into the sunniest, hottest patch of ground you have. Chillies and some sweet peppers (check the packet for the size) also do well in pots on the patio or windowsill.

MAINTENANCE

Keep plants well watered and fed, especially those in pots. Help pollinate plants grown indoors by spraying them with water when they are flowering.

The branches of varieties with large fruits, and even those without, can get overladen and benefit from being tied into a stake. Starting at the cane, mentally divide the branches into three sections, and loop the twine around each section in turn, returning to loop round the cane between each one. Tie off the twine at the cane. Do this about 15cm/6in above soil level when the plant is 30cm/12in high, and again at 30cm/12in high once the plant is 40–50cm/16–20in high.

HARVEST

Peppers will be ready to harvest from midsummer, depending on the variety and when it was sown. A pepper is mature when it feels firm to a gentle squeeze, and can be picked then, even if it is green. For the best flavour wait until the pepper is ripe, when it will be its final colour.

Use in:
• Chilli jam (page 142) • Sweet chilli dipping sauce (page 144) • Pumpkin chutney (page 150) • Tomato ketchup (page 128) • Giardiniera (page 138)

Chilli jam

The joy of making your own chilli preserves is that you have complete control over how hot they are. Not only can you add more or less chilli as you prefer, but you can also grow and use chilli peppers of your desired heat rating and flavour. The recipe below is for a mild(ish) jam that's perfect with goats' cheese, but goes with just about anything.

MAKES ABOUT 450G/1LB

INGREDIENTS
- 375g/13oz tomatoes
- 4–5 garlic cloves, unpeeled
- glug of olive oil
- 6 red chillies, cored, deseeded and finely chopped (leaving the white pith will make the final jam hotter – remove it if you prefer)
- 1½ lemons, juiced
- ¾ tsp fine sea salt
- 4½ tbsp balsamic vinegar
- 140g/5oz light muscovado sugar
- 5 tbsp honey

METHOD
- Preheat the oven to 180°C/350°F/gas mark 4.
- Toss the tomatoes and garlic cloves in the olive oil and put into a roasting dish so that they fit snugly. Roast for 30 minutes until they are soft and the scent of the garlic is wafting out of the oven.
- Remove from the oven and pop the garlic cloves out of their skins.
- Blend the chillies, tomatoes and garlic pulp together until smooth and then pour into a saucepan.
- Stir in the lemon juice, salt and vinegar and bring to a simmer over a medium heat.
- Add the sugar and honey, stirring to dissolve them, and continue to simmer, stirring regularly, for 45–60 minutes until it is reduced and can be parted in the base of the pan.
- Pour into warm, sterilized jars and seal.

Store in a cool, dry, dark place; once opened, keep in the refrigerator
Keeps for a year or more; once opened, lasts for 3–4 months

Grow
- Chillies (page 140)
- Tomatoes (page 124) • Garlic (page 121) • Citrus: lemons (page 101)

Sweet chilli dipping sauce

Ubiquitous in the Thai section of the supermarket shelves, sweet chilli sauce is actually incredibly easy to make yourself. Plus you can use your favourite chillies for the best flavour and heat, making it the perfect sauce just for you. Drizzle it over a curry and rice, or simply dip your favourite crackers or other savoury biscuits into it.

MAKES ABOUT 230G/8OZ

INGREDIENTS
- 5 red chillies, cored, deseeded and finely chopped
- 5 garlic cloves, crushed
- 250ml/9fl oz cider vinegar
- 1 orange, juiced
- 150g/5oz granulated sugar

METHOD
- Put all the ingredients into a medium saucepan. Stirring to dissolve the sugar, bring the mixture to a simmer over a low–medium heat.
- Simmer until the sauce is much reduced and syrupy.
- Pour into warm, sterilized jars or bottles.

Grow
- Chillies (page 140)
- Garlic (page 121)
- Citrus: oranges (page 101)

Store in a cool, dry, dark place; once opened, keep in the refrigerator
Keeps for two months or more

Growing sweetcorn

The clue is in the name: *sweet*corn. This is another of those crops that really benefits from being home-grown, because you can cook it within minutes of picking, unlike sweetcorn cut by farmers, even with all their fancy bits of enormous machinery that process the corn in the field. In a good summer, you can be overrun with cobs, making them perfect for preserving.

BEST VARIETIES

There are some super-sweet varieties available, such as 'Earlibird', but the less sweet ones have more flavour, perform better in temperate climates and are still vastly sweeter than anything you could get from the shops. 'Swift' and 'Sundance' are both reliable performers, while baby varieties such as 'Blue Jade' (with blue/black kernels) and 'Minipop' are suitable for container growing.

PLANTING

Sweetcorn likes well-drained, light soil in full sun. It also benefits from being sheltered from strong winds, if it is to pollinate well (see below).

Station sow sweetcorn in late spring, putting two or three seeds per station, in a block formation rather than in rows. Space the plants 35cm/14in apart in rows 45cm/18in apart. Such block planting significantly enhances pollination rates, because sweetcorn is wind-pollinated, and the breeze shakes the pollen from the male tassels at the top of the plant down to the female flowers. Covering each station with half a plastic bottle as a mini-cloche gets the plants off to a good start – remove the bottle once the plant is pushing against the top. Thin to one or two seedlings per station.

Seeds can also be sown in modules – preferably root-trainers or old loo-roll inner tubes to give the roots plenty of space.

MAINTENANCE

Sweetcorn does not need much water until the cobs start to form, and even then will require only a few good soaks. Keep weeds down, or else plant in a 'three sisters' formation. In this old space-saving method, the following three crops are planted together: sweetcorn; a weed-suppressing mat of pumpkins or other winter squashes beneath; and climbing beans, which scramble up the sweetcorn. Alternatively, omit the beans for a 'two-sisters' approach.

HARVEST

In late summer and early autumn as the tassels turn brown, test each cob for readiness by piercing a kernel with your nail. If it is ripe, it will exude a milky liquid. Pull the cob off the plant with a twisting motion.

Use in:
- Sweetcorn relish (page 146)

Sweetcorn relish

No barbecue is complete without a jar of this relish. The pepper does not have to be red, but it does make the finished relish more colourful.

MAKES ABOUT 800G/1LB 12OZ

INGREDIENTS
- 3 large or 4 medium sweetcorn cobs
- 1 red sweet pepper, cored and deseeded
- 4 shallots
- 500ml/17½fl oz cider vinegar
- 150g/5oz granulated sugar
- 2 tbsp cornflour
- 2 tsp fine sea salt
- 2 tsp mustard powder
- ¼ tsp turmeric

METHOD
- Bring a large pan of salted water to the boil then add the cobs. Cook for 3 minutes, then remove them from the water and cut off the kernels.
- Finely dice the pepper and shallots to pieces approximately the same size as the sweetcorn kernels, then mix with the sweetcorn.
- Put the remaining ingredients in a large pan and whisk to combine and dissolve them over a low heat.
- Bring to the boil, then add the vegetables.
- Simmer for 25–30 minutes until the sauce is thickened and coating the vegetables.
- Scoop off the scum and pot into warm, sterilized jars.

Grow
- Sweetcorn (page 145)
- Sweet peppers (page 140)
- Shallots (page 129)

Store in a cool, dry, dark place; once opened, keep in the refrigerator
Keeps for a year or more

Growing pumpkins and other winter squash

Autumn is my favourite season. I love the colours in the leaves, the fabulous frosty but sunny mornings, and the bounty of fruit and vegetables that are harvested at this time. My kitchen windowsill is not complete without a collection of pumpkins and squashes – until they all get cooked and eaten that is.

BEST VARIETIES

Although of course you can eat them, avoid the pumpkins grown more for Halloween carving than their culinary prowess. Instead opt for varieties that are well known for their great flavour, such as 'Crown Prince' and 'Kabocha', although really it comes down to personal taste so trial your own choices. For jamming, there is actually a specific Italian variety, 'Zucca da Marmellata' (literally, jam pumpkin), but 'Bonbon' would be a good substitute. Check that the growing habit fits your site: trailing varieties need space but can be tied up to strong trellis or stakes with adequate hammock supports for the fruit; other varieties have bushy habits.

PLANTING

All pumpkins and other winter squash need a long, warm summer and early autumn to grow well and ripen properly before the autumn frosts arrive. Sow seeds under cover in modules in mid-spring, potting on before planting out in early summer once all frosts have passed. The plants need an open, sunny, warm site with rich, well-drained soil and at least 1sq m/ 11sq ft of space per plant (unless you are training them upwards).

MAINTENANCE

Water well at the roots, especially in dry periods and as the fruit begins to swell. If a plant produces a lot of baby fruits, cut off the smaller ones to leave around three per plant, to ensure those left develop to a decent size. Place the fruits on pieces of slate, or even chicken wire suspended over two bricks, to ensure they do not rot where they are in contact with the ground.

Tie in plants trained on vertical supports regularly, just under a leaf axil each time. Suspend old pairs of tights or netting bags beneath the fruits to avoid the vine breaking under the weight.

HARVEST

Do this once a fruit has coloured all over and sounds hollow when tapped – but always harvest before the first frosts or the remaining fruits will rot. For the best flavour, and to store into winter, cure the pumpkins or other winter squashes by placing them on a cool, sunny, dry windowsill for at least a month.

Use in:
- Pumpkin jam (page 149)
- Pumpkin chutney (page 150)

Pumpkin jam

Roasting the pumpkin first really intensifies the flavour of this jam. You could also use any other type of winter squash if you don't have pumpkin. Like the Carrot jam (see page 114), this preserve is lightly spiced and is my favourite autumnal alternative for filling a Victoria sponge cake.

MAKES ABOUT 1.2KG/2LB 10OZ

INGREDIENTS
- 2kg/4lb 7oz pumpkin, halved or cut into large sections and deseeded
- 10g/½oz unsalted butter
- 700g/1lb 8oz granulated sugar
- 2 oranges, juiced
- 1 tsp mixed spice
- 1 tsp ground ginger
- large pinch of salt

METHOD
- Preheat the oven to 180°C/350°F/gas mark 4.
- Roast the pumpkin by putting the pieces skin-side down on a baking tray and covering with foil. Cook for 45–60 minutes, until soft. Remove from the oven and leave to cool.
- Scoop the roasted pumpkin flesh out of the skins. Blend 900g/2lb of the flesh to a smooth purée.
- Melt the butter in a large saucepan over a low–medium heat, then add the puréed flesh and stir until heated through.
- Stir in the sugar, orange juice, spices and salt and keep stirring until the sugar is dissolved. Bring to a gentle, plopping simmer and cook until the jam is thick and parts easily at the base of the pan.
- Pot into warm, sterilized jars.

Grow
- Pumpkins and other winter squash (page 148)

Store in a cool, dry place
Keeps for a year or more

Pumpkin chutney

This is probably the chutney I am most proud of in this book. With its sweet pumpkin (or squash) flesh, and just a hint of heat from flecks of red chilli, it is perfect with a mature cheddar and just about every other kind of sandwich you can think of.

Store in a cool, dry place
Keeps for a year or more

MAKES ABOUT 1.2KG/2LB 10OZ

INGREDIENTS
- 2kg/4lb 7oz pumpkin/squash, deseeded and cut into large pieces
- 200g/7oz onions, finely diced
- 1 tbsp olive oil
- 1 red chilli, cored, deseeded and finely chopped
- 200g/7oz raisins
- 400g/14oz light muscovado sugar
- 500ml/17½fl oz cider vinegar
- ½ tsp black pepper

METHOD
- Preheat the oven to 180°C/350°F/gas mark 4.
- Put the pumpkin pieces on a baking tray and cover with foil. Roast for around 30 minutes, until the flesh just yields to the point of a table knife – if for any longer, the pieces will disintegrate too much in the final cooking. Remove from the oven and leave to cool.
- Put the onions and oil into a large pan over a low heat and fry them very gently while you prepare the other ingredients.
- Chop 1kg/2lb 3oz of the roasted pumpkin flesh into cubes of 1cm/½in or smaller. Add these and the remaining ingredients to the onions in the pan and mix together thoroughly.
- Simmer gently over a medium–low heat for around 2 hours, or until the contents of the pan can be parted on the base and there is no free liquid.
- Pot into warm, sterilized jars and store for 2 weeks before using.

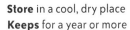

Grow
- Pumpkins and other winter squashes (page 148)
- Onions (page 129)
- Chillies (page 140)

Growing herbs

A herb patch is an invaluable addition to any cook's garden: the ability to use really fresh herbs brings another dimension to any culinary effort, including preserving. The herbs detailed here are just the basic ones for adding flavour to various preserves, as well as those that can be preserved in their own right. I would encourage you to seek out and plant as many different herbs as you can.

BASIL
(*Ocimum basilicum*)

Annual. Assorted varieties are available, from classic sweet basil to other flavoured leaves. A sunny spot in rich soil is ideal, including in pots, and basil makes a good companion plant for carrots and tomatoes. Sow seed in spring and in successive batches until late summer, but do not plant outside until early summer, once there is no risk of frost. Pinch out the growing tips of seedlings, to encourage branching. Water in dry periods, especially to avoid bolting. Pick the leaves as required until the first frosts.

Use basil in
• Pesto (page 158)

BAY
(*Laurus nobilis*)

Evergreen shrub. Grow in a sunny, warm area of the garden or in a large container. Buy plants, which are available relatively cheaply when small; larger specimens are often trained as standards. Bear in mind that the smaller the plant the less use you will get out of it for a while, because bay trees are not fast growers. Water as required, and feed plants in pots throughout the growing season. Pick off leaves as needed.

Use bay in
• Bramble jam (page 72) • Pickled garlic (page 122)
• Horseradish sauce (page 160)

CHIVES
(*Allium schoenoprasum*)

Herbaceous perennial. Buy plants, or start from seed. Chives will grow well in most situations, including moister soils and shadier positions than the Mediterranean herbs (rosemary, thyme and their ilk). Plants require cutting back only once the foliage has died down in autumn. However cutting back after flowering as well will produce a fresher head of leaves for the rest of the summer. Garlic chives are also a good investment. Cut leaves from the base as needed (flowers also edible).

Use chives in
• Pesto (page 158)

CORIANDER
(*Coriandrum sativum*)

Annual. Sow and grow as for basil (see left). Varieties include those specifically for leaf ('cilantro'), because many others tend to go to seed rapidly (bolt). However if it is the seeds you want, such bolting is no problem. Harvest the seeds when they have dried to brown, and dry further by storing in a paper bag in a cool, dry place before putting into an airtight jar.

Use coriander in
• Pickled rhubarb (page 110) • Beetroot chutney (page 118) • Giardiniera (page 138)

DILL
(*Anethum graveolens*)
Annual. Sow as for basil (see opposite). Grow in partial shade to prevent dill from bolting too early; when this does occur, remove the flower stems. Cut leaves as needed.

Use dill in
• Pickled cucumber (page 134)

FENNEL
(*Foeniculum vulgare*)
Herbaceous perennial. Plant in full sun (it will tolerate a little shade). Cut the leaves as needed. Harvest the seeds, to prevent them germinating all over the garden, and save them for culinary use if desired. Cut back the dead stems in autumn/winter.

Use fennel in
• Herb and flower syrups (page 164) • Giardiniera (page 138)

HORSERADISH
(*Armoracia rusticana*)
Herbaceous perennial. Horseradish will grow well in most soils and is happy in partial shade. This vigorous plant is virtually impossible to eradicate once it has established, so give some thought as to where you plant it in the garden. Alternatively put horseradish in a large pot raised on feet to ensure the roots do not spread downwards into the ground (they can penetrate brick and paving). Buy potted plants or 'thongs' (pieces of root) and plant in spring. Harvest the roots year-round, as required, but they are at their most pungent from mid- to late autumn. Dig out what you need and leave the rest.

Use horseradish in
• Horseradish sauce (page 160) • Red chrain (page 120)

LEMON VERBENA
(*Aloysia citrodora*)
Tender deciduous shrub. Buy in pots and plant out into a sunny border or larger container. The latter is better if you need to move the plant under cover for winter – it will just about survive outside in temperate climates if in a sunny, free-draining position and it is given a mulch in autumn to insulate the roots. Regular picking keeps the plant to size (unchecked and in a good spot it will easily reach 2.5m/8ft tall and wide). Prune in spring to re-establish a good framework of branches if necessary. Pick leaves as required.

Lemon balm (*Melissa officinalis*) makes an acceptable, fully hardy, substitute to lemon verbena and also has a lime variety – *M. officinalis* 'Lime Balm'. Grow as for mint (see page 156), although the roots will not spread.

Use lemon verbena in
• Herb and flower syrups (page 164) • Blueberry conserve (page 62)

MINT
(*Mentha*)

Herbaceous perennial. Tolerates partial shade and prefers damp, well-drained soil. Many different flavoured cultivars are available including peppermint, chocolate mint, spearmint and strawberry mint. Grow in a pot or where you do not mind the plant spreading – the stems will readily root along the ground. Cut back after flowering for fresher leaves in late summer and autumn, then cut back the dead stems in late winter. Pick leaves as required.

Use mint in
• Herb and flower syrups (page 164) • Herb and flower jellies (page 162) • Raspberry jam (page 53)

NASTURTIUMS
(*Tropaeolum majus*)

Annual. Nasturtiums will grow in any soil in a sunny position. Bushy or spreading varieties are available; the latter are good for trailing over the edge of raised beds or hanging baskets but they can reach more than 1.5m/5ft long. Sow seeds in mid-spring in modules or station sow; and plant out in late spring. Water as required, and remove the dead plants in winter. Pick the leaves when needed. The flowers are also edible, but let some develop into seeds.

Use nasturtium in
• Pesto (page 158) • Pickled nasturtium seeds (page 161)

OREGANO/MARJORAM
(*Origanum*)

Herbaceous perennial. Plant in a pot or sunny spot in well-drained soil. Assorted varieties are available, including compact plants. Cut back the dead stems in winter. Pick leaves as required; the flowers are also edible.

Use oregano and marjoram in
• Herb and flower jellies (page 162) • Pickled garlic (page 122)

PARSLEY
(*Petroselinum crispum*)

Annual/biennial. Moist soil and a sunny position are ideal, although parsley tolerates a little shade. Flat leaf or curly varieties are available. Sow in spring and in successive batches until late summer (the leaves will overwinter if given protection from a cloche or tunnel). This herb makes a good companion plant for carrots and onions. Pick leaves as required and remove plants once they start flowering.

Use parsley in
• Pesto (page 158)

ROSEMARY
(*Rosmarinus officinalis*)

Evergreen shrub. Buy as potted plants and put into a sunny position in well-drained soil. Upright and compact varieties are available that are suitable for container growing. Snip off stems as needed, and remove flowered stems in early summer. Try and resist taking too many stems in the first year. If you allow the plant to reach a good size before picking, it will reward you with stronger growth and bigger harvests for longer. Plants live for many years, but are often best replaced after five.

Use rosemary in
• Herb and flower jellies (page 162) • Herb and flower syrups (page 164) • Rhubarb and rosemary ketchup (page 112) • Giardiniera (page 138)

SAGE
(*Salvia officinalis*)

Evergreen shrub. Plant and grow as for rosemary (see opposite). Pick leaves as required; such harvesting helps keep the plant from sprawling everywhere.

Use sage in
• Herb and flower jellies (page 162) • Apple chutney (page 82)

THYME
(*Thymus vulgaris*)

Evergreen shrub. Assorted varieties available, the best of which are the basic culinary thyme and lemon thyme. Plant and grow as for rosemary (see opposite), but pick leaves as required and cut back after flowering to help keep the plant from sprawling everywhere.

Use thyme in
• Herb and flower jellies (page 162) • Herb and flower syrups (page 164) • Caramelized onion marmalade (page 130)

WILD GARLIC
(*Allium ursinum*)

Bulbous perennial. Plant in dappled shade and moist soil (it thrives in woodlands). Sow seed or plant bulbs, either dry in autumn or in the green during spring. Remove the flowers of wild garlic, also known as ransoms, to prevent self-sowing, if desired. Cut the leaves as required; the flowers also are edible.

Use wild garlic in
• Pesto (page 158)

Always cut herb sprigs just above a lower set of leaves or branches.

Pesto

Home-made pesto is a different beast to the jars in the shops: it is punchier, and the individual ingredients more obvious than in the smooth sauces you can buy. By growing a variety of different leaves, you can make fresh pesto year-round. Use the basic recipe for the quantities, then refer to the variations below for the different leaves and so on to substitute for each one.

Something a little different

BASIL
Use basil (*Ocimum basilicum*) leaves and pine nuts, and include the garlic cloves.

CARROT TOPS
Use only the youngest, thinnest leaves (not the stalks) from the carrots, together with pine nuts and garlic cloves.

CHIVES
Use chives (*Allium schoenoprasum*) with pine nuts and garlic cloves, unless you use garlic-flavoured chives (in which case omit the garlic cloves).

NASTURTIUMS
Use nasturtium (*Tropaeolum majus*) leaves, pine nuts and garlic cloves.

PARSLEY
Use parsley (*Petroselinum crispum*) leaves and walnuts and include the garlic cloves.

WILD GARLIC
Use young wild garlic (*Allium ursinum*) leaves, pine nuts or hazelnuts, but omit the garlic cloves.

MAKES ABOUT 220G/8OZ

INGREDIENTS
- 25g/1oz nuts
- 100g/3½oz fresh leaves
- 1 garlic clove, crushed (optional, see variations, left)
- ½ lemon, zest
- 50–100ml/1½–3½fl oz extra-virgin olive oil
- 50g/2oz Parmesan cheese, finely grated
- salt and pepper, to taste

METHOD
- Toast the nuts in a dry frying pan over a medium heat until aromatic, moving them constantly (this will take 5 minutes or less).
- Put the nuts with the fresh leaves, garlic clove (if using) and lemon zest into a food processor and pulse until the leaves are finely chopped. Add 50ml/1½fl oz olive oil and blitz further to a paste.
- Stir in the cheese and then season with salt and pepper.
- Pack into sterilized jars, then add more olive oil to cover the top with an oil layer 0.5–1cm/¼–½in thick. This will help preserve the pesto and keep it from browning. Add more oil over the top every time you take out some pesto.

Note: You can add more oil to the pesto to your desired consistency, especially if you are using it straight away. However because the pesto is stored with oil in the jar, I find it easier (and more economical on oil) to use less in the pesto itself, because extra is inevitably scooped up from the preservation layer when you take it out of the jar. Getting the pesto to the right consistency and then storing it with more oil makes it oilier than Popeye's best gal.

Store in the refrigerator
Keeps for a month or more;
    once opened, lasts for a few weeks

Grow

• Basil (page 154) • Carrots (page 113)

• Chives (page 154)

• Nasturtiums (page 156)

• Parsley (page 156)

• Wild garlic (page 157)

Horseradish sauce

For some, a roast beef dinner is not complete without horseradish sauce. It is easily one of the most pungent, intense condiments around and, as you might expect, it's better to stay upwind of the grated root as far as possible! The sauce is actually made in two stages: first the raw root is preserved in vinegar, then when it is required some of the horseradish is scooped out and mixed with a creamy base to form the actual sauce.

Note: Read the recipe through and prepare all your ingredients and utensils before you start to avoid any potential discoloration of the horseradish, which can occur once it is peeled.

Grow
• Horseradish (page 155)
• Bay (page 154)

Store in the refrigerator
Keeps for six months or more

MAKES ABOUT 225G/8OZ OF PRESERVED HORSERADISH

INGREDIENTS
Preserved horseradish:
- 300ml/½ pint white wine vinegar
- ½ tbsp black peppercorns
- 1 bay leaf
- ½ tbsp granulated sugar
- 1 tsp salt
- 600ml/1 pint water
- 200–250g/7–8oz horseradish root (a medium to large one)

Horseradish sauce:
- 3 tbsp preserved horseradish
- crème fraîche or double cream, whipped (see method)
- pinch of mustard powder
- salt and pepper, to taste
- 1 lemon, juiced (optional)
- caster sugar, to taste (optional)

METHOD
- **For the preserved horseradish**, put the vinegar, peppercorns, bay leaf and sugar into a small saucepan and bring to a gentle simmer, stirring to dissolve the sugar. In a separate saucepan, stir the salt into the water until dissolved, then bring to the boil and remove from the heat. Peel the horseradish and immediately grate it directly into the hot, salted water. This prevents it from browning. Once it is all grated, drain it through a sieve and pat dry with clean kitchen paper. Pack the grated horseradish into warm, sterilized jars and pour over the strained vinegar, then seal immediately.
- **For the horseradish sauce**, scoop out the preserved horseradish (leave the vinegar behind) and stir through crème fraîche or double cream to your desired consistency. Stir in a pinch of mustard powder and the salt and pepper. If you want a smooth sauce, blend it all together. You could also add lemon juice and/or, as is recommended in *The Closet of Sir Kenelm Digby Knight Opened* of 1669, a 'very little sugar, not so much as to be tasted, but to quicken (by contrariety) the taste of [the horseradish]'.

Pickled nasturtium seeds

'Poor man's capers' is the other name for pickled nasturtium seeds, and it could not be more accurate: the little green seeds do taste remarkably like capers once preserved (they are OK raw, but better pickled). As a bonus, harvesting the green seeds means you are less likely to have nasturtiums cropping up where you don't want them next year. The quantities here are deliberately non-specific to allow for as many or as few jars as you are able to fill from your plants.

MAKES AS MUCH AS YOU LIKE

INGREDIENTS
- enough green nasturtium seeds to fill your jar(s)
- fine sea salt
- white wine vinegar

METHOD
- Wash the seeds in a sieve under cold running water. Put them into a bowl and cover with water, then drain, measuring how much water was needed to cover the seeds. Leave the seeds to dry on a clean tea towel.
- Make a brine using a pinch of salt to every tablespoon (15ml/0.5fl oz) of water it took to cover the seeds in the bowl. Stir the salt into the water until it is dissolved.
- Put the dry seeds back into the original bowl with the brine and cover. Leave at room temperature for 24 hours.
- Drain the seeds through a sieve and rinse under cold running water, and again leave to dry on a clean tea towel.
- Tip the seeds into a sterilized jar(s), and pour over enough white wine vinegar to cover them completely, tapping the base of the jar(s) gently on the work surface to release any trapped air bubbles.
- Seal and store for 3 weeks before eating. (I prefer to rinse the seeds before using them.)

Grow
- Nasturtiums (page 156)

Store in a cool, dry, dark place
Keeps for six months or more

Herb and flower jellies

As an accompaniment to a roast dinner, a savoury jelly is an excellent thing (alternatively, whisk a spoonful into the gravy). Sweet jellies can be served by the spoonful with a plain biscuit and some Earl Grey tea. Crab apples are a great base for these jellies, but cooking apples are a fine substitute in the savoury ones and actually better for the flowers and sweet herbs. The best herbs for these jellies are the really aromatic ones such as rosemary (*Rosmarinus*), thyme (*Thymus*), sage (*Salvia*), mint (*Mentha*), lavender (*Lavandula*) and rose (flowers).

MAKES ABOUT 500G/1LB 2OZ (USING CRAB APPLES); ABOUT 900G/2LB (USING COOKING APPLES)

INGREDIENTS
- 1kg/2lb 3oz crab apples, halved, or cooking apples, roughly chopped
- large bunch of flowers/herbs
- granulated sugar (100g per 150ml/3½oz per ¼ pint of juice; see method)
- 75ml/2fl oz cider vinegar (for savoury jellies only)
- small bunch or a few sprigs of herbs/flowers, finely chopped (optional)

METHOD
- Put the apples into a large pan with the bunch of herbs and just enough water to cover the fruit.
- Cover the pan with a lid and bring to a gentle simmer over a low–medium heat and cook until the fruit is very soft.
- Mash thoroughly with a potato masher, then tip the entire contents of the pan into a jelly bag.
- Hang up the bag and leave it to drip for at least 3 hours, preferably overnight.
- Discard what is left in the jelly bag. Measure the juice into a clean pan with the appropriate amount of sugar and (if a savoury jelly) the vinegar. Heat gently, stirring to dissolve the sugar.
- Once it is dissolved, bring to the boil and boil rapidly until it reaches a setting point (see Testing for a set, page 32).
- Stir in the finely chopped leaves if you are using them; if so, leave the mixture to stand for 5 minutes before stirring again and potting into warm, sterilized jars. Alternatively pot straight away and poke in a small sprig of the herb or flower into the top of the pot, ensuring it is completely submerged in the jelly.

Grow
- Apples and crab apples (page 76) • Herbs (page 154)
- Flowers (page 166)

Store in a cool, dry, dark place
Keeps for a year or more

Herb and flower syrups

These syrups are simple and quick to make and are easily the best way to preserve the essence of an individual herb or flower. The quantities below give enough to drizzle over a cake, pudding or ice cream, or to make a round of drinks (try them in cocktails or mocktails as well as a cordial substitute). This recipe works for any herb or edible flower you can think of – sweet or savoury – but my favourites are rose, elderflower (*Sambucus nigra*), lemon verbena (*Aloysia citrodora*), scented pelargonium, blackcurrant leaf and lemon thyme (*Thymus citriodorus*).

MAKES ABOUT 150ML/¼ PINT

INGREDIENTS
- 100g/3½oz caster sugar
- 100ml/3½oz water
- handful of herb leaves or edible flowers

METHOD
- Put the sugar into a small saucepan with the water and, over a low–medium heat, stir to dissolve the sugar, then bring to the boil.
- Reduce the heat and simmer for 5 minutes (uncovered).
- Take the pan off the heat and add the herb leaves or flowers. Stir to coat them in the syrup, then cover the pan and leave it to infuse for at least 30 minutes, and preferably 1½ hours.
- Strain the syrup through a sieve into a jug, pressing the flowers/herbs to extract every last drop of flavour.
- Pour into warm, sterilized bottles.

Grow
- Herbs (page 154)
- Flowers (page 166)
- Blackcurrants (page 49)

Store in a cool, dry, dark place; once opened, keep in the refrigerator
Keeps for a month or more

Growing flowers

Many flowers are edible, and deserve more recognition in the kitchen. The ones described here are my favourites to use as flavourings or to preserve as syrups, jams and jellies in their own right. They can all also be included in scented sugars (see Making scented sugars, page 29).

ELDERFLOWER
(*Sambucus nigra*)
Large, deciduous shrub or small tree. Grows in most soils and situations. It can make a pretty garden shrub, and is easily managed by pruning hard when necessary. The UK native *S. nigra* is ubiquitous in hedgerows and scrubland, both rural and urban, largely because birds love the berries and scatter the seed everywhere. Other species – there are black-leaved and pink-flowered types too – also have edible flowers. If you forage for the flowers, start scouting locations in late spring, but avoid dusty roadsides and other potentially polluted flowers. Growing your own can avoid this hazard. Pick heads that have three-quarters of the flowers open and are in full sun for the best flavour, but do not take them all – leave some to develop into berries for yourself or the birds. Always cook both flowers and berries.

Use elderflower in
• Gooseberry jam (page 41)
• Herb and flower syrups (page 164)

LAVENDER
(*Lavandula angustifolia*)
Evergreen shrub. When cooking, always use *L. angustifolia*, rather than French or butterfly lavender (*L. stoechas*), which is poisonous. Any of the cultivars of *L. angustifolia* can be chosen, such as the more compact 'Hidcote' for smaller sites. Buy potted plants and put into a sunny position and well-drained soil. Harvest the flower spikes just as the lowest buds on the spike begin to open; tie them in bunches and hang upside down to dry before rubbing the flowers off the stems and storing in an airtight container. To avoid the plants becoming straggly shorten all the stems after flowering, making sure you leave some green growth. Replace lavender bushes every five years.

Use lavender in
• Herb and flower jellies (page 162) • Herb and flower syrups (page 164) • Blueberry conserve (page 62)

HEDGEHOG ROSE
(*Rosa rugosa*)
Deciduous shrub. Grows in most soils in full sun or partial shade. Although other roses such as dog rose (*R. canina*) and the *moyesii* hybrid *R.* 'Geranium' produce good hips, hedgehog rose's excellent flavour in both flowers and hips means it is the most efficient choice for a herb garden. Standalone plants reach about 1.5m/5ft in height and spread. Hedgehog rose is a slightly untidy-looking plant so is best put in a mixed border if you want only one or two bushes. It makes a good hedge too – plant 60cm/2ft apart for this. The flowers are deep pink, but there is also a white form ('Alba'), and a magenta pink ('Rubra'). Aside from taking off the tips of each stem and removing any dead wood in late winter, hedgehog roses need no pruning. Pick the flowers as required, but leave some from mid- to late summer to develop into hips, which will be ready when just softening and a deep orange-red. Always cook the hips first (see Rosehip syrup, page 168) because they contain millions of tiny hairs that badly irritate the throat if eaten raw. If you are harvesting from a friend's garden, make sure they have not sprayed their flowers.

Use roses in
• Herb and flower syrups (page 164) • Herb and flower jellies (page 162) • Rosehip syrup (page 168)

SCENTED PELARGONIUMS (*Pelargonium*)

Tender, evergreen subshrub. In cool-temperate climates grow in pots as houseplants for a sunny windowsill in winter, moving them outside for the frost-free part of the summer. In warmer areas they can be grown outside in pots or the open ground year-round: they will prefer well-drained soil and full sun. The leaves of these plants come in a huge range of the most amazing perfumes, from rose to lemon to nutmeg and more, but all develop the distinctive pelargonium base. The citrus and rose scents are my favourites – 'Attar of Roses' is one of the best for a rose fragrance, and there are many lemon, lime and orange varieties to choose from. Cut back to a good framework of stems about 15cm/6in high in spring, and repot every couple of years. Pick the leaves as needed; you can use the flowers too.

Use scented pelargoniums in
• Herb and flower syrups (page 164)

SWEET VIOLETS (*Viola odorata*)

Evergreen perennial. This low-growing plant favours moist soil and shade, and makes excellent ground cover under fruit bushes. Buy as potted plants and double-check you are getting the right plant, and not another *Viola*. Small, purple flowers are borne in late winter and early spring. Other than an optional tidy up of the leaves in summer, sweet violet plants need no maintenance. They like to spread and colonize, so be sure you want them where you plant them.

Use sweet violets in
• Herb and flower syrups (page 164)

Rosehip syrup

The *Good Housekeeping Complete Book of Home Preserving* (1981) recommends rosehip syrup 'as a pleasant way to improve a diet lacking in vitamin C'. Make this syrup then dilute a teaspoonful or two with hot water (or add it to a cocktail) for a great winter drink. Hedgehog rose (*Rosa rugosa*) hips give the best flavour, but any rosehips could be used.

MAKES ABOUT 200ML/7FL OZ

INGREDIENTS
- 100g/3½oz rosehips, de-stalked and cleaned
- 280ml/9fl oz water
- 60g/2oz granulated sugar

METHOD
- Very finely chop the rosehips, using a food processor if you have one.
- Bring 160ml/¼ pint of the water to boil in a small saucepan, then add the chopped hips.
- Bring it back to the boil, then remove the pan from the heat. Leave it to stand (covered) for 20 minutes.
- Strain the entire contents of the pan through a jelly bag, leaving it until it stops dripping – do not squeeze the bag. Set aside the juice.
- Put the pulp that remains in the jelly bag back into the saucepan with the remaining cold water. Bring it to the boil, then remove the pan from the heat and leave to stand (covered) for 15 minutes.
- Clean the jelly bag and then strain the contents of the pan through it and leave it to drip, but this time discard the pulp once it has stopped dripping.
- Combine the two lots of juice in a clean saucepan over a medium heat and add the sugar, stirring to dissolve it.
- Bring it to the boil and boil for 4 minutes, then pour into warm, sterilized bottles. Because this syrup does not keep long once opened, use several small bottles rather than one large one if you are making it in quantity. Shake the bottle before using as the syrup separates out in storage.

Store in a cool, dark place; once opened, keep in the refrigerator
Keeps for nine months or more; once opened, lasts for about a week

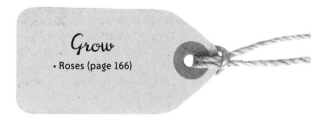

Grow
- Roses (page 166)

Further resources

The RHS is an excellent resource for any gardener: www.rhs.org.uk. Members can also send or take in samples for plant or pest and disease identification, and soil composition tests.

Useful books for reference and inspiration:
- *RHS Vegetable and Fruit Gardening* edited by Michael Pollock (Dorling Kindersley, 2012)
- *RHS Grow for Flavour* by James Wong (Mitchell Beazley, 2015)
- *RHS Pests and Diseases* by Pippa Greenwood and Andrew Halstead (Dorling Kindersley, 2009)
- *Creating a Forest Garden* by Martin Crawford (Green Books, 2010) is the definitive work on incorporating edible plants into all levels of a garden
- *The New Kitchen Garden* by Mark Diacono (Saltyard Books, 2015)
- *The Flavour Thesaurus* by Niki Segnit (Bloomsbury, 2012)

It is also worth seeking out kitchen gardens. Many have tasting days at which you can try different varieties of fruits and vegetables before you buy, and experts on hand to offer growing advice as well.

You can contact me on twitter, @Holly_E_Farrell

Index

Acknowledgments

No author works alone, and there are a lot of people without whom this book would not have been possible. I really enjoyed creating this book, and am very grateful to Helen Griffin and Andrew Dunn of Frances Lincoln for the opportunity to do so. Joanna Chisholm and designer Becky Clarke once again joined the team to put the whole thing together, and Laura Nicolson put up with my endless emails. Thank you all.

Turning a humble garden cookbook into a thing of beauty once again fell to Jason Ingram and, once again, he surpassed all my expectations. Despite spending several days photographing almost all the jams in this book, we had only one sticky moment: when he asked me (for the sake of the image) to go against a lifetime's worth of scone eating and put the jam on top of the cream. It is a testament to Jason's unerring eye and exquisite taste that I allowed this to happen. Thank you.

Rupert and Liz Lywood, thank you again for your generosity, it is enormously appreciated. I'd also like to thank Bedstone Blueberries, the Ludlow Cookshop, South Devon Chilli Farm, Thompson & Morgan and Yorkshire Flowerpots

My family – Mum, Rich, Elle and Ollie – never flinched when presented with a table full of jars for tasting, so thank you all for being ready and willing to grab a spoon.

I think, given the choice, my darling husband would prefer I didn't write books that created huge piles of washing up. However he keeps schtum and is always incredibly supportive and encouraging: Kevin, thank you.

Last, but by no means least, is our wonderful daughter, who despite being only one year old displayed immense patience when Mummy had to work, and helped out with some excellent stirring as well. Thank you!

Frances Lincoln Limited
A subsidiary of Quarto Publishing Group UK
74–77 White Lion Street
London N1 9PF

The Jam Maker's Garden
Copyright © Frances Lincoln Limited 2017
First Frances Lincoln edition 2017
Text copyright © Holly Farrell
Photographs copyright © Jason Ingram,
except for p13 bottom © GAP Photos/Robert Mabic
Edited by Joanna Chisholm
Designed by Becky Clarke Design
All rights reserved.

A catalogue record for this book is available from the British Library.

ISBN 978-0-7112-3814-5

Printed and bound in China

9 8 7 6 5 4 3 2 1

MIX
Paper from
responsible sources
FSC® C104723

Quarto is the authority on a wide range of topics.

Quarto educates, entertains and enriches the lives of our readers – enthusiasts and lovers of hands-on living.

www.QuartoKnows.com